FOLLOWING THE LAW

The Total Tricks Sequel

by

Larry Cohen

Natco Press 1994

FOLLOWING THE LAW

The Total Tricks Sequel

by

Larry Cohen

Edited by Susie Cohen

Thanks to:

Marty Bergen, David Berkowitz, Neil Cohen, Paul Cohen, Jim Houser, Robin Kay, Karen McCallum, Bill Pollack and Steve Weinstein

ISBN No. 0-9634715-4-6

Library of Congress Catalog Card Number: 94-067961

FOLLOWING THE LAW

The Total Tricks Sequel

Table of Contents

FOREWORD
by David Berkowitz

Playing bridge with a matinee idol is no easy task.

At bridge tournaments day and night, in all corners of the world, deep thought is often interrupted by, "Larry Cohen, I must show you a hand." Naturally it is a hand where the LAW ostensibly does not work, and just as naturally, whatever we are doing stops as Larry patiently explains what has gone wrong.

To Bid Or Not To Bid has been very good to me (and Larry, too!). The book has created such an innovative way of looking at competitive bidding, that Larry is in great demand all over the world. As his partner, I feel it is my duty to accompany him on these junkets, to protect him from his admirers. It is a tough job, but somebody has to do it.

When Larry and I started playing seriously several years ago, he said that there were only two rules for this partnership. Rule 1 was no yelling (of course, my wife defines yelling as me raising my eyebrows, but Larry is a bit more tolerant). Rule 2 was that I must be dedicated to the LAW of Total Tricks. My response was, "What in the world is that?" I didn't know.

Larry taught me well, and the rest, as they say, is history. My first violation of the LAW, in a misguided attempt to push around my opponents, was greeted by a whispered "tsk tsk" from Larry, which for him is the equivalent of screaming at the top of his lungs. I have since vowed to keep my partner happy, but every once in a while I feel the urge . . .

It turns out that usually when I have these urges, I tell Larry that I "violated the LAW" because I had so many points in their suit, or because I thought there was a double fit. Larry says that I'm not violating the LAW, I'm simply "adjusting." Now, when Larry's readers claim that the LAW has seemingly failed them, I know the answer. I realize that the LAW is not breaking down, but more accurately, the players are breaking the LAW. They are not properly adjusting or evaluating their cards in conjunction with the LAW.

I told Larry what needed to be done. The first book, instructive as it was, needed elucidation. Larry had to write another book and further explain the intricacies of adjusting.

Unfortunately, his readers' gain will be our loss. As bridge players obtain better and better judgement via utilization of the LAW, it becomes that much more difficult for us to win.

Such is the price of fame.

Enjoy your experiences with the LAW. I know I have.

David Berkowitz
August, 1994

Chapter 1 - The LAW (1968-2018)

1968 . . . Paris, France

Jean-René Vernes, the discoverer of the LAW of Total Tricks, is perplexed. "Quel dommage! Why didn't you raise me to the three level? You knew we had nine trumps. Sacré Bleu. Some day the world will learn about my LAW!"

1993 . . . Reisinger Teams, Seattle.

"LAR - RY CO - HEN ! ! !"

The voice shattered the deep concentration of the room.

It was unmistakably the voice of Zia, the mercurial Pakistani star. The implication was clear. Zia had gotten a poor result, and the LAW of Total Tricks was to blame. There was nobody to complain to but the arch defender of the LAW, poor old me.

The knowledgeable group of players in the room was chuckling. This was no private joke. It was 1993, and everybody knew about the LAW.

Here was the deal that upset Zia:

```
Dlr: South        ♠ Q 9 4 3
Vul: None         ♡ Q 8 4 2
                  ◇ 9 7 4
                  ♣ 9 7
    ♠ K 7 5 2                    ♠ J 10 6
    ♡ J 3                        ♡ 6 5
    ◇ A K 5 3                    ◇ J 10 8 2
    ♣ K 10 2                     ♣ A Q J 6
                  ♠ A 8
                  ♡ A K 10 9 7
                  ◇ Q 6
                  ♣ 8 5 4 3
```

South	West	North	East
Rosenberg	Shugart	Zia	Silverman
1♡	Dbl	3♡ *	Dbl **
Pass	Pass	Pass	

* Weak
** Responsive

Zia was playing against my teammates, Rita Shu-
gart and Neil Silverman. Zia's partner, Michael
Rosenberg, opened the South hand with a bid of one
heart. After Shugart's double, Zia followed the
LAW, and bid to the nine-trump level, three hearts.
Silverman made a responsive double to show that he

had a reasonable hand, but no long suit to bid.

Shugart now had a chance to make a LAWful decision. She reasoned that her side had at best an eight-card fit and that there were at most 17 trumps on the deal. This indicated that it was wrong to go on to the four level. She made a gutsy pass and ended up +100 after collecting a spade trick and two tricks in each minor suit.

Zia was blaming me. In the old days he'd have pushed his unknowing opponents into four diamonds, down one. In the 1990's, obedient players abide by the LAW and don't bid to the four level unless there are enough trumps.

2018 . . . Pan Polar Simultaneous Teams, South Pole - viewgraph room

"He's kicked the LAW and he will pay!" The voice is that of Chuck Goren III, chief commentator. "What in the world was he thinking about?"

Looking around the room, I expected a lot of icy blank stares. There were none. After all, this was 2018, and references to the LAW were as common as references to quick tricks and high-card points.

"Take a look at these half-time statistics."

	Glaciers	Arcadians
Unforced errors:	-22	-18
Winners:	+16	+21
Good slams bid:	+23	+13
ASTRO usage:	-11	-13
LAW violations:	-17	-44

Goren continued, "The Arcadians are losing heavily on LAW violations. When will these people ever learn?"

Chapter 2 - Reviewing the LAW

Learning the LAW. The basics were explained in *To Bid or Not to Bid,* but I think a brief review will lay a good foundation for the rest of this book.

We start with the definition of the LAW of Total Tricks:

> **The <u>Total Number of Tricks</u> available on any deal is approximately equal to the <u>Total Number of Trumps</u>.**

Total Number of Tricks means the combined total tricks available to *both* sides (assuming best play and defense) if they play in their best (longest) fit. For example, if North-South can take **9 tricks** in their 5-4 (longest) spade fit, and East-West can take **8 tricks** in their 4-4 (longest) diamond fit, then the total number of tricks would be **9**+**8**, or **17**.

Total Number of Trumps means the combined total of cards in *both* sides' best trump fit. In the above example, North-South's best (longest) fit is a 5-4 spade fit, and East-West's best (longest) fit is a 4-4 diamond fit. Thus, the total number of trumps is **9**+**8**, or **17**.

The full deal might look like:

```
                    ♠ Q 10 5 2
                    ♡ A Q 3
                    ◇ A 3
                    ♣ 10 9 7 2
    ♠ 7 6                          ♠ 8 3
    ♡ 8 6 4 2                      ♡ K 7 5
    ◇ K Q 10 8                     ◇ J 6 5 4
    ♣ K Q 3                        ♣ A J 6 4
                    ♠ A K J 9 4
                    ♡ J 10 9
                    ◇ 9 7 2
                    ♣ 8 5
```

North-South have **9** spades, and East-West have **8** diamonds for a total of **17** trumps.

North-South can take **9** tricks (losing one heart, one diamond, and two clubs). East-West can take **8** tricks (losing two spades, two hearts, and the ace of diamonds). The total number of tricks is **17**.

It is no coincidence that the 17 trumps are equal to the 17 tricks. What about that losing heart finesse? Well, there is no need for concern. The beauty of the LAW is that the number of tricks is predicated solely on the number of trumps, not the location of the high cards. Look what happens if we put the king of hearts into the West hand:

```
                    ♠ Q 10 5 2
                    ♡ A Q 3
                    ◇ A 3
                    ♣ 10 9 7 2
    ♠ 7 6                           ♠ 8 3
    ♡ K 6 4 2                       ♡ 8 7 5
    ◇ K Q 10 8                      ◇ J 6 5 4
    ♣ K Q 3                         ♣ A J 6 4
                    ♠ A K J 9 4
                    ♡ J 10 9
                    ◇ 9 7 2
                    ♣ 8 5
```

Now the heart finesse wins for North-South, and they can take **10** tricks in spades. The total number of trumps is still **17**, so we expect that the number of tricks should also be **17**. Is it?

East-West now have an additional loser. They will lose *three* heart tricks, along with the same two spade losers and the ace of diamonds. They can take only **7** tricks. The total number of tricks is still **17**, this time **10**+**7**.

Two questions should spring to mind:

1) Will this "trumps = tricks" work out exactly on every deal? No. There is a lot more to the LAW than its definition, as we'll soon see. Adjustments (the subject of Chapter Four) are the key to the LAW.

2) How does this "trumps = tricks" information help us in a bridge game?

That question was the subject of *To Bid or Not to Bid*. I further fine-tune it in this book, and after reading both books, I hope you'll be an expert in Following the LAW.

The simplest rule that results from the LAW is:

> **You should strive to compete to the level of the number of trumps held by your side.**

This means that if your side has eight trumps, you should bid to the two level. With nine trumps you are safe at the three level, and so on. This was the subject of an article I wrote for the Bols Royal Distilleries. The tip was called "Eight Never - Nine Ever," and it appears in Appendix A at the back of this book.

This rule also provides a corollary:

> **Try not to let the opponents play at a level equal to their number of trumps.**

If you think your opponents have eight hearts, you should not let them play in two hearts.[1]

All of your competitive bidding should be structured around the above two concepts.

A more advanced way of looking at the LAW is also quite useful. I refer to it as "chart logic." This stems from the making of a "mental chart" to see what you should bid, based on how many trumps you think there are.

This "chart logic" is essential to understand. However, before you think in "chart terms," you must make some determination from the bidding as to how many trumps you think there are. (I know, this won't always be easy!)

For example, with both sides vulnerable you hold:

♠ K 8 7　♡ J 5 3　◇ K 7 2　♣ Q 9 6 5,

and hear the following auction:

---

[1] If they have nine cards, they are safe on the three level, but it won't always be easy for you to compete (you might not have enough of a fit).

♠ K 8 7 ♡ J 5 3 ◇ K 7 2 ♣ Q 9 6 5
(repeated for convenience)

LHO	Partner	RHO	You
1♡	1♠	2♡	2♠
3♡	Pass	Pass	??

You expect that your side has eight trumps. You won't have nine, because partner, with six spades, would have bid to the three level himself -- he'd know your side had nine trumps.

The opponents only have eight trumps. If your partner had a singleton heart, he would probably have bid three spades, expecting them to have nine.

Expecting eight trumps for both sides, you will eventually know that you should not bid "three-over-three." For now, let's use this setup to explore "chart logic," which will be employed throughout the book.

We have eight and they have eight, for a total of 16 trumps and 16 tricks.

Here's the all-important chart:

CHART FOR 16 TRUMPS - BOTH VUL.

We play the hand in three spades		They play the hand in three hearts	
Our # of Tricks	Our Score	Their # of Tricks	Our score
10	+170	6	**+300**
9	+140	7	**+200**
8	-100	8	**+100**
7	-200	9	**-140**

On the first line the 16 tricks are split 10 for us and six for them. On the left side it shows +170, the score for three spades making 10 tricks, not as much as the +300 we'd get for defending against three hearts. On the second line the scores for a nine-seven division of the tricks are shown, and so on. Look carefully at the scores that result from our bidding three spades. No matter how the 16 expected tricks are divided, the boldfaced right-hand side (they play in three hearts) will produce a better score for us.

Using "chart logic," this means that we should pass and let them play in three hearts.

The chart tells us that bidding on to three spades with only 16 trumps is not a winning proposition. In particular, note the line where each side can take eight tricks. This happens to be the most likely occurrence when the points are fairly evenly divided between both sides and there are only 16 trumps. In this scenario, neither partnership can make a three-level contract, and passing three hearts will produce +100, while bidding "three-over-three" will result in -100.

The full deal might be something like:

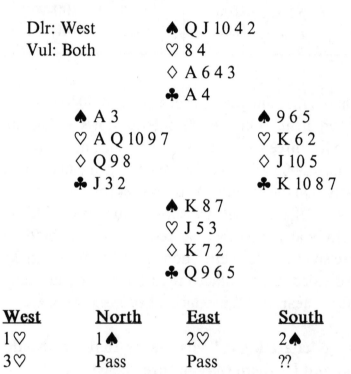

Dlr: West		♠ Q J 10 4 2	
Vul: Both		♡ 8 4	
		◇ A 6 4 3	
		♣ A 4	

♠ A 3			♠ 9 6 5
♡ A Q 10 9 7			♡ K 6 2
◇ Q 9 8			◇ J 10 5
♣ J 3 2			♣ K 10 8 7

		♠ K 8 7	
		♡ J 5 3	
		◇ K 7 2	
		♣ Q 9 6 5	

West	North	East	South
1♡	1♠	2♡	2♠
3♡	Pass	Pass	??

Both sides have eight tricks; bidding three spades would be a losing proposition for South.

The definition, along with the "chart logic," are the fundamentals of the LAW. However, the real benefits go to those readers who also understand adjustments. Because many players didn't read Chapter Nine[2] of *To Bid or Not to Bid*, I always seem to hear the following:

"Larry, look at this hand . . . " I know what's coming. Someone is running up to show me that the LAW failed them. "Look, there were 17 trumps and 19 (or 20, or 23, or 29!) tricks -- what's wrong with your LAW?" I think to myself, "it's not *my* LAW, and I never said it's perfect anyway."

I also wonder, "Did they read Chapter Nine?" "Seventeen trumps, and nineteen tricks," they sneer. Trying to be polite -- after all, everyone is a potential book buyer! -- I look at the full deal:

---

[2] This "Major Adjustment" chapter was put near the end of *To Bid or Not to Bid* because of its technical nature. In this book, I've learned the error of my ways, and I'm addressing this crucial subject at the outset!

```
              ♠ A Q 10 x
              ♡ K J x
              ◇ x x x
              ♣ x x x
  ♠ x x x                    ♠ x
  ♡ x x x x                  ♡ x x
  ◇ K Q x                    ◇ A J 10 x x
  ♣ 10 x x                   ♣ K Q J 9 x
              ♠ K J 9 x x
              ♡ A Q 10 x
              ◇ x x
              ♣ A x
```

The first thing I notice is that the deal looks rigged. Look at those beautiful double fits. Look at all those working honor cards. Everything looks so nice and neat.

North-South have 10 top-tricks in spades, and East-West have nine easy winners in either minor. Yes, there are 19 tricks, and indeed, only 9 + 8 = 17 trumps. How can this be? Should we rewrite the LAW?

When you have finished reading Chapter Four, I suggest you review this deal again. You'll then know that there are "positive adjustment factors" hard at work. The positive adjustment factors lead to the extra tricks, and that comes as no surprise to LAW experts.

Can you can make the LAW work out exactly on every deal by adjusting?

Even though many accuse me of trying to do so, the answer is still NO! It is not necessary for LAW users to be stubborn and insist that every deal is just one more example of the LAW working perfectly. That would be silly.

Unfortunately, not everyone sees the benefits of the LAW. There exists a group of players that is anti-LAW. They are insulted by the idea that this "LAW" can be better than their impeccable bidding judgment. They even object to my using capital letters to call it the LAW! They're the ones that are so quick to point out the deals where the LAW doesn't work. Even after adjusting, such deals still do exist.

Why does it bother me that people seem to take glee in pointing out these unLAWful deals? Because it's ridiculous! With any bridge bidding method, you can make a similar fatalistic contention. You can take a popular convention like Stayman or Blackwood and show a deal where it doesn't work out.

Even the point-count system has its flaws. When people started counting high-card points in the 1930's, there must have been some player who held the following hand:

♠ Q 7 ♡ 10 8 2 ◇ K Q 4 3 ♣ K J 7 2.

His partner opened one notrump, showing 15-17 of these new things called "high-card points." He diligently counted his own hand, and with 11 high-card points he triumphantly raised to three notrump. Alas, his partner's hand was:

♠ J 5 ♡ A K 6 5 ◇ A 8 5 2 ♣ A 9 4.

His opponents cashed five spade tricks for down one. Was the point-count system worthless? No, it just didn't work on every deal.

Of course, time and repetition proved that counting high-card points was the way to go. Although it doesn't work on all deals, it unquestionably works on the majority of them.

The LAW of Total Tricks won't work on every bridge deal you play. Every now and then the LAW will look silly, as will you. People will no doubt continue to run up to me when it fails, while taking for granted all the hands where it works.

In the 1990's we're all pioneers of the LAW, just like there were pioneers for the 4-3-2-1 point-count system in the 1930's and 1940's. Don't be dissuaded when the LAW fails you. The number of trumps will not exactly equal the number of tricks on every deal. The LAW is a guideline -- not a quadratic equation.

Chapter 3 - Applying the LAW

Let's put our LAW review into action.

With both sides vulnerable at IMPS you hold:

♠ K 8 7 6   ♡ K 5 3   ◇ K 10 7 2   ♣ K J,

and hear the following auction:

You	LHO	Partner	RHO
1◇	1♡	Dbl*	2♡
2♠	3♡	Pass	Pass
??			

* Negative

Your partner's negative double showed four spades, so your side has eight trumps. If your partner had a singleton heart, there is an excellent chance he'd have bid three spades over three hearts on his own. So, partner rates to have a doubleton heart, and we can assume that the opponents also have eight trumps.

At some point you'll be able to solve this problem with a rule, such as "with eight trumps for both sides, don't bid three-over-three." For now, I suggest using

29

"chart logic." This is the exact same situation as the deal on page 20, and you can use the same chart as on page 21.

The full deal (16 trumps - eight per side) might be something like:

```
Dlr: South        ♠ A Q 9 4
Vul: Both         ♡ 8 4
                  ◇ Q J 5
                  ♣ 10 9 6 3
    ♠ J 10                      ♠ 5 3 2
    ♡ A 10 7 6 2                ♡ Q J 9
    ◇ 8 6 4                     ◇ A 9 3
    ♣ A Q 4                     ♣ 8 7 5 2
                  ♠ K 8 7 6
                  ♡ K 5 3
                  ◇ K 10 7 2
                  ♣ K J
```

South should choose to defend against three hearts, and he'll end up +100. East-West have only eight tricks in hearts, losing two tricks in spades and diamonds and one in clubs. Had South violated the LAW, he would have been -100 in three spades, losing two tricks in hearts and clubs and the ace of diamonds. The chart logic clearly shows the way.

Every now and then I play at my hometown bridge club where I was first exposed to duplicate play. The players all knew me when I was a little kid, and now they rush over to me. "Oh, you've done so well . . . , " or "I remember when I used to be your partner . . . , " or more recently, "I loved your book on the LAW." I love to hear that, but I wonder if they've really digested what I had to say. Unfortunately, many people who read *To Bid or Not to Bid*, were impressed and fascinated at the moment, but soon thereafter went back to their old ways. They *should* know the LAW, but they kind of forget to use it! Kind of the same way I react to the golf lessons I take. Sounds good on the practice range, but then I go out on the course and hit the same bad shots.

At that childhood club, I was recently handed a top because one of those admirers who "loved the book" violated the LAW. With both sides vulnerable, she held:

♠ A K Q 10 x ♡ Q 9 x x ◇ x x x ♣ x.

She heard me open the bidding with one diamond, and her partner passed. My partner responded one heart, and she made the normal overcall of one spade. I bid two hearts, followed by two spades by her partner. My partner bid three hearts, although he didn't know how many hearts I had for my raise.

In most of my partnerships I play "support dou-bles[3]," and my two-heart raise guarantees four-card support. However, on this occasion I was playing with a friend who was unfamiliar with that conven-tion, and my two-heart bid showed either three or four-card support.

Larry	North	Larry's partner	LAW Admirer
1◇	Pass	1♡	1♠
2♡ (3 or 4)	2♠	3♡	??

You, dear reader, are hopefully thinking that this is a non-problem. If so, you have a good understand-ing of the LAW. (Or you have good instincts.) Un-fortunately, most players' instincts tell them to bid three spades, which is exactly what this South player did. She envisioned heart shortness in her partner's hand, and figured she could score several tricks by ruffing hearts in dummy.

Instead, she should have realized that her partner had only three spades. (With four spades, her part-ner should have been bidding to the three level!) If the defenders led trumps, and they probably would

---

[3] There are many bidding methods designed to utilize the LAW. These were covered in *To Bid or Not to Bid*, and *Better Bidding with Bergen*, Volumes I & II. For a brief review of these methods, please refer to Appendix B.

have many chances, what was she going to do with all of her hearts?

Looking at it LAWfully, her side has eight trumps, and the opponents have *at most* eight. Don't bid "three-over-three" with "eight-and-eight!" As it turns out, her opponents had only seven trumps, and this was the rather unfortunate dummy that she caught:

♠ J 9 x ♡ 10 x ◇ J 9 x ♣ K Q 10 9 x.

Granted, this was a big disappointment, but even opposite a more cheery:

♠ J 9 x ♡ x ◇ K x x x ♣ K x x x x,

she would still be in danger of -200 after a trump lead. This was the full deal:

Dlr: West   ♠ J 9 x
Vul: Both   ♡ 10 x
                 ♢ J 9 x
                 ♣ K Q 10 9 x

```
        ♠ x x x              ♠ x x
        ♡ A x x              ♡ K J x x
        ♢ A K Q 10           ♢ x x x
        ♣ J x x              ♣ A x x x
```

               ♠ A K Q 10 x
               ♡ Q 9 x x
               ♢ x x x
               ♣ x

Larry	North	Larry's partner	LAW Admirer
1 ♢	Pass	1 ♡	1 ♠
2 ♡ (3 or 4)	2 ♠	3 ♡	3 ♠
Pass	Pass	Pass	

She was -200; the defense took three diamonds, two hearts and the ace of clubs. She would have done quite well defending against three hearts, collecting possibly four tricks in the black suits and two trump tricks.

I hated to have to raise to two hearts with the West hand; I would have much preferred a support double after one spade to show three-card heart support. We were on shaky ground at the three level without any eight-card fit. However, as is usually the case, you can get away with it if the opponents are LAW violators who bail you out of trouble by bidding one more themselves.

When I play in weak fields, I often see some unusual things. Even on the silliest of deals, I still find myself thinking about the LAW. For example, I held:

♠ J x x ♡ K x x x ◇ K J x ♣ K x x.

Vulnerable against not, my partner dealt and opened with a weak two-heart bid. This was followed by a pass, and it was my call. I know that you might consider me a hypocrite if I didn't bid four hearts -- after all, I should expect 10 trumps!

However, at unfavorable vulnerability, not to mention being four-triple-three, some discretion was called for. I contented myself with a preemptive raise to three hearts, and my left-hand opponent mulled things over and eventually passed. My partner passed, and against inexperienced opponents I might have expected to hear a balancing bid on my right.

Of course, LHO's huddle did not bar my RHO. However, a hand that passed on the first round was unlikely to be able to act over three hearts, especially since RHO had to bend over backwards to ignore the fact that his partner's tempo seemed to indicate values. So, he duly passed (forgive me for even thinking that he might do something unethical!), and three hearts became the final contract.

The opponents led spades, and partner ruffed the second round. While I'm the dummy, I like to keep myself entertained. So, as you might have guessed, I started thinking about how many total trumps and tricks were available on this deal. Since my partner had one spade, and presumably six hearts, it looked like there were 10 hearts for us and nine spades for them. It didn't take any fancy math to figure out that we had to be getting a great score for playing on the three level when there were 19 trumps. In fact, see if you can construct the other three hands, giving partner six hearts and one spade, and try to come up with a layout where three hearts would lead to a bad result. Good luck!

The full deal isn't important, but I just wanted to point out that you don't have to sit there being bored when you are the dummy. Furthermore, I hope you won't be caught defending a three-level contract when there are 19 trumps!

Playing in a sectional mixed pairs with your significant other, you hold:

♠ A 5 4 2   ♡ 7 3   ◊ J 8 4   ♣ J 10 7 2.

Nobody is vulnerable, and you hear three clubs on your left, three hearts by partner, and four clubs on your right. You pass this back to partner, who doubles for takeout. This is the decision you are faced with:

LHO	Partner	RHO	You
3♣	3♡	4♣	Pass
Pass	Dbl	Pass	??

If you're not a LAW user, you will have to rely on your instincts and judgment. (The same stuff that usually gets me in trouble with my mixed partners away from the table!) You'd probably assume partner's shape is something like 3-6-3-1 or 4-6-3-0, and you might decide to bid four hearts or four spades. Alternatively, you might like your J10xx of clubs and decide to pass.

If you think carefully about the LAW, this type of problem becomes easy. You expect the opponents to have eight or nine trumps, while your side probably has eight trumps. (If you pull the double, it's not clear whether you would choose to bid four hearts or four spades, but in either case you're probably not going to have more than eight trumps.) As they have

37

eight or nine trumps and you have eight, you know that there are at most 16 or 17 total trumps, and therefore, 16 or 17 tricks. What does this tell us?

If we were to bid four-of-a-major and were fortunate enough to take 10 tricks, how many tricks would the opponents have? To make the total 16 or 17, they would have six or seven. If we have only nine tricks, we'd expect them to have seven or eight. Isn't it easy to see that there are simply not enough trumps or tricks to bid four-of-a-major? This problem is not a problem if you know the LAW. This is what the full deal looked like:

Dlr: West   ♠ K Q 9 8
Vul: None   ♡ A K 10 9 5 4
                  ◇ K 10 7
                  ♣ --

   ♠ 6   ♠ J 10 7 3
   ♡ Q 8 6   ♡ J 2
   ◇ 9 6 5   ◇ A Q 3 2
   ♣ K Q 9 8 6 4   ♣ A 5 3

                  ♠ A 5 4 2
                  ♡ 7 3
                  ◇ J 8 4
                  ♣ J 10 7 2

West	North	East	South
3♣	3♡	4♣	Pass
Pass	Dbl	Pass	??

In the sectional, many South's faced with this problem chose to bid four spades. They found this contract too difficult to handle after the normal club lead. They ruffed in dummy and just couldn't manage to take 10 tricks. North-South didn't have enough trumps!

The South's who passed four-clubs doubled defeated it one or two tricks. They usually took one spade, two hearts, one diamond, and one club trick -- especially after the start of ace, king, and another heart.

Even though the deal is a bit complicated to analyze, the theme comes through loud and clear. There were not enough trumps for both sides to be trying to take 10 tricks. There were 17 trumps and approximately 17 tricks. Not enough to bid four-of-a-major over four clubs!

Chapter 4 - Adjusting the LAW

In *To Bid or Not to Bid*, the toughest problem for me, the writer, was what to do about adjustments. Just the word "adjustments" seemed like it would be enough to scare away any casual reader. Who wants to be bothered? Unfortunately, what I refer to as "adjustments" are really vital ingredients of the LAW. I stuck adjustments at the back of the first book so that I wouldn't lose too many readers.

Adjustments are really the key to a lifetime of good bidding decisions. If you learn to use adjustments correctly, you'll be able to evaluate hands like the world's best players do.

Simply put:

To derive the full benefits from the LAW, you must be familiar with adjustments!

"Adjusting," in reality, is just a different way of describing what most experts call "hand evaluation."

Let's consider the following: A one-diamond opening bid is doubled by your partner and raised to two diamonds by your right-hand opponent. You're looking at:

♠ 9 x x x ♡ K J x ◇ Q J x ♣ x x x,

with nobody vulnerable. Would you bid two spades? Maybe, maybe not. Now suppose instead that you had a similar-looking seven-count:

♠ Q J 9 x ♡ K J x ◇ x x x ♣ x x x.

After hearing the same auction, you'd now be pleased to bid two spades. What's the difference? You realized that the second hand, with the queen-jack in your own suit, as opposed to theirs, was a much better hand for competing with two spades. In LAW terms, we would say that you "adjusted."

The first hand had two *negative adjustment factors* -- "minor honors" in the opponents' trump suit (QJx of diamonds), as well as a lack of same in your own suit (9xxx of spades). The second hand was much more "pure." The "minor honors" are in your suit (QJ9x of spades), and nothing is wasted in their (xxx of diamonds).

Let's look at the two types of adjustments:

POSITIVE AND NEGATIVE ADJUSTMENTS

Negative Adjustment Factors (Suggest Total Tricks will be **less** than the number of trumps)	Positive Adjustment Factors (Suggest Total Tricks will be **greater** than the number of trumps)
1) **Negative Purity** minor honors in opponents' suits and/or <u>poor</u> interiors in your own suits	1) **Positive Purity** <u>no</u> minor honors in opponents' suits and/or <u>good</u> interiors in your own suits
2) **Negative Fit** misfits	2) **Positive fit** double/double fit
3) **Negative Shape** flat hands	3) **Positive Shape** extra length or voids

We use the information in this chart to help us make our bidding decisions. We look at our hand and try to determine if there are negative or positive adjustment factors present. After making that determination, we will adjust our estimate of the total number of trumps/tricks upwards or downwards. The upshot of all this is that:

43

> **When there are Negative factors:**
> **We will tend to pass or double.**
>
> **When there are Positive factors:**
> **We will tend to bid on.**

Let's say we are confronted with a bidding problem and have gone through all the LAW fundamentals as reviewed in Chapter Two. We've estimated from the bidding that there are 16 trumps. But, before we make our bidding decision, we should do a quick check for adjustment factors.

If there are only negative factors, we will expect fewer tricks than trumps. If there are only positive factors, we will expect more tricks than trumps. However, if both are present, we expect trumps to equal tricks; the negative and positive factors cancel each other out.

Although adjusting is not an exact science, the presence of these factors will help you "lean" in one direction or the other. On many hands you won't know whether to choose 16 or 17 as the number of trumps. If there are more negative factors than positive ones, then use 16 as your estimate. If more positive factors exist than negative ones, then use 17 as the number of tricks.

Since these factors will alter our total trick count, let's look through the chart and see how we can recognize its components.

NEGATIVE FACTORS:

The first and most important negative factor is "minor honors." This term can be a bit confusing since, in bridge terminology, "minors" often refer to clubs and diamonds. Of course, in this context, "minor" has nothing to do with suit denomination!

What we mean by "minor honors" are holdings that will often provide a trick on defense, but not on offense. The ace of the opponents' suit would not be a minor honor. You'd expect it to be a trick no matter which side plays the hand. It won't influence the *total* trick count.

However, holdings such as Qxx or QJx are considered to be "minor honors." We could easily take a trick on defense with either holding if the suit is trump. Instead, if we were playing the hand in our own trump suit, our holding of Qxx or QJx of their suit could easily be useless. Opposite two small, we'd have to lose to the ace and king. Maybe our queen would set up for a useful discard, but probably not. These holdings have a definite effect on the *total* trick count and that effect is a negative one.

Here is a list of typical minor-honor combinations. If you have any of these holdings in the opponents' trump suit, you should be wary about competing. They should cause you to adjust your total-trick appraisal downwards.

Minor honor holdings

AJxx	AJx
KQx	KQ
K10xx	K10x
KJxx	KJx
Kx	K
Q10xx	Q10x
QJxx	QJx
Qxxx	Qxx
Qx	Q
J10xx	Jxxx
Jxx	Jx

"Poor interiors in our suit" is also a negative sign. A trump holding of J 6 4 3 2 is much more "negative" than J 10 9 6 3. Lack of the 10's and/or 9's of your side's trump suit is often a reason to lean towards defending in a close situation.

The second negative adjustment factor listed is "misfits." If, from the bidding, you can tell that neither side rates to have a fit (eight or more cards), the total trick count should be adjusted downwards. This factor occurs infrequently and is not very important.

The third and last negative adjustment factor listed is "flat hands." This refers to balanced hands -- hands without singletons or voids, typically 4-3-3-3 or 5-3-3-2. If you have a flat hand and you are in doubt as to how many trumps/tricks there are, then assume the lower number. This also is not a very important adjustment factor.

POSITIVE FACTORS:

Positive factors, as you might have guessed, are basically just the opposite of negative factors. (Refer back to the chart on page 43.) Positive purity, the first positive adjustment factor, is the possession of good interiors in our suits and lack of "minor honors" in the opponents'. With pure hands, the number of tricks is often higher than expected. Pure hands generally argue for bidding as opposed to passing.

Our second positive factor, double fits, is the opposite of misfits. For LAW purposes, when "BOTH SIDES HAVE AN 8+ CARD FIT IN TWO DIFFERENT SUITS," there is a double fit. Actually, it would be more correct to call it a "double/double fit." When we see that a double fit exists, we will expect more tricks than the number of trumps.

47

Our third and last positive factor is the presence of voids and long suits. These factors are often over-looked. It is important to realize that voids usually lead to extra tricks. As well, seven-card suits (or longer) are a very powerful trick-taking weapon.

"Larry," you ask, "does this mean that every hand has adjustments? You have to have "minor honors" in your suit or their suit -- so it seems like we'll be forever adjusting!" That's a very good question which can be answered by looking at this typical deal:

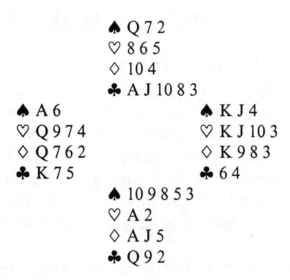

```
              ♠ Q 7 2
              ♡ 8 6 5
              ◇ 10 4
              ♣ A J 10 8 3
♠ A 6                        ♠ K J 4
♡ Q 9 7 4                    ♡ K J 10 3
◇ Q 7 6 2                    ◇ K 9 8 3
♣ K 7 5                      ♣ 6 4
              ♠ 10 9 8 5 3
              ♡ A 2
              ◇ A J 5
              ♣ Q 9 2
```

North-South have eight spades, and can take eight tricks in a spade contract (losing three trump tricks and one in each red suit). East-West have eight hearts and also have eight tricks (losing one heart trick and two in each minor suit). What about the adjustments?

East's spade holding is a negative factor ("minor honors" in his opponents' suit), and indeed, it reduced the trick count. To see this, mentally interchange East's jack of spades with one of North's small ones. Now, North-South will take nine tricks in a spade contract, but East-West will still take only eight in hearts. There would be 17 tricks, but only 16 trumps. In that case, the deal would be very pure; in both the spade and heart suits there would be no "minor-honor" holdings.

Now, on the original deal, let's also consider the double fit. North-South have eight of each black suit, while East-West have eight of each red suit. That usually produces an extra trick. Why doesn't it produce one in the diagram? Because the jack of spades and the diamond suit are working against the double fit. The ◇ AJx opposite ◇ 10x yields two tricks on defense against a heart contract, but produces only one trick on offense in spades. The "negativity" of the diamond and spade honors offsets the double fit.

So, on this deal, like on most deals, there are several adjustment factors pulling in opposite directions. On most deals there will be one or two on "each side of the chart," and tricks will exactly equal trumps. When there are only positive factors (or more positive than negative), there will be extra tricks; the reverse is true for excessive negative factors.

By how many tricks should you adjust? Look again at the chart on page 43. All the positive factors on the right-hand side, and #1, "minor honors," on the left-hand side, are of roughly the same importance. The other two negative factors (#2 and #3) don't need to be given much weight. Most often, the important factors will balance out, and if not, they usually lead to a one or two-trick adjustment. From the examples throughout this book, you'll be able to gauge how much these factors affect the trick count. However, for now I would recommend this guideline:

If there is an **equal** number of negative and positive factors, then make no adjustment.

If the **positive factors** slightly outweigh the negative ones, then consider adding one trick to the total-trick count. If there are many positive factors and no negative ones, then add at least one, possibly two tricks.

If the **negative factors** slightly outweigh the positive ones, then consider subtracting one trick from the total-trick count. If there are many negative factors, and no positive ones, then subtract at least one, possibly two tricks.

It pleases me to see that bridge writers now analyze deals using the LAW of Total Tricks. Yet, it annoys me to no end when they ignore adjustments. Edgar Kaplan, publisher of the esteemed *Bridge World* magazine, wrote about this deal from the 1993 World Championships:

```
Dlr: North        ♠ A 10
Vul: None         ♡ K J
                  ◇ J 9 7 3
                  ♣ Q J 9 7 5
    ♠ 9 7 6 2                    ♠ Q J 5 4
    ♡ 8 7 6 2                    ♡ --
    ◇ Q 10                       ◇ A K 8 6 4
    ♣ A 3 2                      ♣ K 10 8 6
                  ♠ K 8 3
                  ♡ A Q 10 9 5 4 3
                  ◇ 5 2
                  ♣ 4
```

On this deal there are 17 trumps; North-South have nine hearts and East-West have eight spades. Are there 17 tricks?

No. North-South have 10 easy tricks in hearts -- two top spades, a spade ruff in dummy, and seven more heart tricks. It's hard to analyze what happens to East-West in spades. Kaplan wrote "my best guess is down one [in four spades], although there are certainly chances of making it."

He then makes me happy by discussing the LAW: ". . . according to the LAW, there are 17 total tricks -- if East-West can make four spades, they will beat four hearts doubled 500, while if four hearts makes then four spades doubled goes for 500. . . ." The deal was played at eight different tables so there were various auctions. East-West often chose to defend against four hearts. As Kaplan pointed out, if East-West deduced 17 trumps from the bidding, the math showed that they shouldn't bid four spades. He even used "chart logic!"

However, as he continued, he got my blood boiling by writing: " . . . Only, there were 19 or 20 total tricks. <u>Illegal</u>!" What an insult to the LAW. He totally ignored adjustments. Of course there were more than 17 tricks; South had a long running suit! All of the South players jumped to four hearts to show their long suit. The East-West "trump-counters" should have known that there would be more than 17 tricks. Long suits produce extra tricks. This is not <u>illegal</u>! It is adjusting.

Any time that you think that the LAW is wrong or "off," it is probably due to adjustment factors. By taking these factors into account, you will find that the LAW is quite legal!

Let's try to solve some competitive problems using the LAW. All of them will involve adjustments, or if you prefer, "good bidding judgment."

As you try the problems, see if you can identify the positive and negative factors in each hand and where they fall on the chart of positive and negative adjustments. For all three problems, assume nobody is vulnerable playing IMPS.

1)

Partner	**RHO**	**You**	**LHO**
1♢	1♡	1♠	2♡
2♠ (4 trumps)	4♡	??	

a)

```
♠ J 9 7 6 2
♡ Q 10 3
♢ J 7 6 4
♣ K
```

b)

```
♠ Q J 9 6 2
♡ 8 7 3
♢ K J 9 4
♣ 3
```

2)

Partner	RHO	You
2♡	Pass	??

a)

```
♠ K 10 4
♡ K 8 7 6
◇ Q J 3
♣ Q J 4
```

b)

```
♠ K 4 3
♡ K J 7 6
◇ Q J 4 3
♣ 5 4
```

3)

LHO	Partner	RHO	You
1♠	2NT *	3♠	??
* minors			

a)

```
♠ K J
♡ Q J 7
◇ 8 7 4 3
♣ 9 5 4 2
```

b)

```
♠ 5 4
♡ 8 7 3
◇ K 8 7 4
♣ Q J 4 2
```

As a LAW user, you should get used to the proper way of thinking about adjustments, so we'll go through each decision.

On problem #1, as with all competitive bidding problems, we start by trying to count the total number of trumps. With hands *a* and *b*, our side has nine spades; we will assume that partner's raise shows four. Many people play that it conventionally promises four. The opponents' bidding indicates their heart fit -- presumably eight or nine cards. That means there are 17 or 18 total trumps.

Let's start our thinking with 18 as the number of total trumps. This means partner has four spades and one heart. With 18 trumps/tricks we would tend to bid four spades since one side will probably be able to make 10 tricks. Bidding would be wrong, and only slightly so, in the case where the 18 tricks were divided nine for each side. That would turn a score of +50 into -50.

But here is where adjusting comes into play. Even though there might be 18 *trumps*, with *a*,

♠ J 9 7 6 2 ♡ Q 10 3 ◇ J 7 6 4 ♣ K,

we wouldn't expect 18 *tricks*. Our heart and possibly, our club holdings scream "minor honors." These holdings will often yield a trick on defense, but not on offense. Further, our lack of intermediates in our suits, spades and diamonds, also screams for a negative adjustment. With 18 trumps there might be only 16 or 17 tricks. We can't put an exact number on the "negativity" of this hand, but we know that we should downgrade from 18 tricks. There won't be enough tricks to warrant bidding four spades.

What if there are 17 trumps? If we decide that partner is 4-2 in the majors, making 9 + 8 = 17 total trumps, *we should not* count on 17 tricks. Since our hand is filled with negative adjustment factors, we must downgrade to 15 or 16 tricks. We shouldn't even be tempted to bid four spades.

Now, with the same auction, let's consider hand *b*:

♠ Q J 9 6 2 ♡ 8 7 3 ◇ K J 9 4 ♣ 3.

Still, we come up with the same 17 or 18 trumps, but now we have positive adjustment factors. First of all, we have a double fit in spades and diamonds, while the opponents might have a fit in clubs as well as hearts. True, this also existed in *a*, but given that our honors are in the spade and diamond suits, doesn't this feel like a better double fit? More importantly, we satisfy the first condition for positive adjustments: We have all of our "minor honor" cards in our side's suits, with none in the opponents'. We should add at least a trick to the trump total. If there are 17 trumps, we can expect at least 18 tricks.

If there are 18 trumps, we can expect at least 19, maybe even 20 tricks. With hand *b*, we have a clear-cut four-spade bid:

<pre>
                    ♠ K 10 8 5
                    ♡ K 4
                    ◇ A Q 3 2
                    ♣ J 9 5
        ♠ A 4 3   ♠ 7
        ♡ 10 6 5   ♡ A Q J 9 2
        ◇ 10 6 5   ◇ 8 7
        ♣ K 10 7 2   ♣ A Q 8 6 4
                    ♠ Q J 9 6 2
                    ♡ 8 7 3
                    ◇ K J 9 4
                    ♣ 3
</pre>

Look how many tricks there are! Eleven for them, nine for us. Twenty tricks, but only 17 trumps (actually, there are 18 trumps if East-West play in clubs). The double fit and purity produce three (two) extra tricks.

Now let's go back to hand *a* and look at a typical full deal:

```
              ♠ K 10 8 5
              ♡ K 4
              ◇ A Q 3 2
              ♣ J 9 5
♠ A 4 3                    ♠ Q
♡ 8 6 5                    ♡ A J 9 7 2
◇ K 9 8                    ◇ 10 5
♣ 10 7 3 2                 ♣ A Q 8 6 4
              ♠ J 9 7 6 2
              ♡ Q 10 3
              ◇ J 7 6 4
              ♣ K
```

Here, the opponents fail by two tricks in four hearts. They still have two diamond losers, but they also have two losers in hearts and one in clubs. No surprise -- your hand suggested that. Your side has at most eight tricks in spades -- notice the slow diamond loser due to your lack of interiors in the suit. Unless declarer guesses to lead a spade to the king, he will lose two trump tricks, plus a trick in each of the other three suits. There will be 8+8 or only 16 tricks. There are 17 trumps (18 if E-W play in clubs) but only 16 tricks. With only 16 tricks, it would be futile to bid four spades over four hearts.

With *a* you should adjust *downwards* to approximately 16 tricks and therefore, **pass**. If there are fewer tricks available, you don't want to declare and go minus. With *b* you should adjust *upwards* to approximately 19 tricks and choose to **bid**. Since there are extra tricks for both sides, you want to buy the contract. You can either call this good LAW usage with adjustments, or good bidding judgment.

Let's try problem #2.

2)

Partner	**RHO**	**You**
2♡	Pass	??

a) ♠ K 10 4 ♡ K 8 7 6 ◇ Q J 3 ♣ Q J 4
b) ♠ K 4 3 ♡ K J 7 6 ◇ Q J 4 3 ♣ 5 4

We expect six trumps from partner, so the LAW ostensibly tells us to bid to the 10-trick level, namely four hearts. But don't you feel uncomfortable bidding four hearts with that unsightly first hand?

Of course you do. This is because of the "minor honors" in all three suits. If partner has

♠ Q 7 ♡ A Q 10 9 4 2 ◇ 7 5 ♣ 8 6 3

your side will have only eight tricks, while the opponents quite possibly have just eight tricks if they play in their spade fit. They could easily have a loser in all three side suits and two trump losers due to your ten of spades. Their probable loser in diamonds translates into a trick for you on defense, but zero tricks in a heart contract! Your ten of spades could also be a trick on defense, but is useless in a heart contract.

You'll also note that you have an additional negative adjustment factor. The third factor in the chart is "flat hands," and your hand definitely qualifies. "Four-triple-three" shape should make you think twice about competing to a high level.

If the opponents are smart enough to double and defend against four hearts, they will collect +300 without having a game their way. The deal contains $10 + 8 = 18$ trumps, but probably only 16 or 17 tricks. Your "minor honors" and flat shape should keep you from bidding four hearts. This is the kind of hand where players who have only an elementary understanding of the LAW might recklessly bid four hearts. They reason: "The LAW says we're safe at the four level with 10 trumps." Not so, if you know how to adjust.

With *b*,

♠ K 4 3 ♡ K J 7 6 ◊ Q J 4 3 ♣ 5 4

it's much safer to raise to four hearts. Now, when partner has the same:

♠ Q 7 ♡ A Q 10 9 4 2 ◊ 7 5 ♣ 8 6 3

the opponents will have a game, losing at most a trick each in spades, hearts and diamonds. For the most part, the negative factors in *a* are no longer present. Your hand is relatively pure, and you have no excuse to do anything other than raise to the ten-trick level.

By now the theme should be familiar.

3)

LHO	Partner	RHO	You
1♠	2NT *	3♠	??
* minors			

In this problem, with *a*:

♠ K J ♡ Q J 7 ◊ 8 7 4 3 ♣ 9 5 4 2,

you should not get carried away with a big preempt to the five level. The full deal could look like:

```
Dlr: West              ♠ Q 7
Vul: None              ♡ 8
                       ◇ K Q J 10 6
                       ♣ K Q J 7 6
     ♠ A 10 6 5 3              ♠ 9 8 4 2
     ♡ A 9 5 2                 ♡ K 10 6 4 3
     ◇ 9 5                     ◇ A 2
     ♣ A 3                     ♣ 10 8
                       ♠ K J
                       ♡ Q J 7
                       ◇ 8 7 4 3
                       ♣ 9 5 4 2
```

Here, the opponents have a loser in each suit and can't make any game. Your side is also off four top tricks. Competing to four-of-a-minor is high enough. Normally, with 18 trumps and a big double fit you'd expect 19 or 20 tricks, justifying a sacrifice in five-of-a-minor. But your honors in both major suits (and lack of same in the minors) should prevent you from competing to the five level. There are 18 trumps and 18 tricks. The double fit is offset by the the possession of your honors in the opponents' suits.

However, with *b*:

♠ 5 4 ♡ 8 7 3 ◇ K 8 7 4 ♣ Q J 4 2,

while you are still assured of a double fit, you no

longer have "minor honors." There are nothing but positive adjustment factors. You expect 18 trumps, but more than 18 tricks. You add tricks for the double fit and the purity. In *a*, you added one for the double fit and subtracted one for the "minor honors," a total of only 18 tricks, so you avoided the five level. Here, with *b*, you do nothing but positive adjusting -- you decide that there are 18+1+1 + ? . . . at least 20 tricks, and you should definitely compete to the five level:

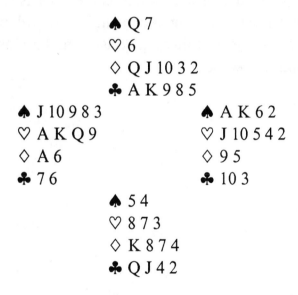

Your save will cost only -300 as opposed to -450 against four spades. There are the same 18 trumps, but thanks to the positive adjustment factors there are 20 tricks (11 for them, nine for us).

In all three examples (and most other bridge problems) it was necessary to adjust. Is there an exact formula for adjusting? No. This is a vagarious card game, not rocket science.

The LAW is a great guideline. Yes, you'll do quite well to bid to the level of the number of trumps your side has. However, you'll do even better if you also try to estimate the number of trumps for *each* side and then take into account positive and negative adjustment factors. While some experts are using their keen "bidding judgment," you will be using your excellent "adjusting skills" to make consistently winning decisions.

Chapter 5 - Using Adjustments

In a regionally rated mixed-pairs event, with both sides vulnerable, you are dealt the following hand:

♠ A Q 5 4   ♡ 6   ◇ J 10 7 4   ♣ 9 8 5 3.

Your partner, the dealer, opens one diamond, to which you respond one spade. After a two-heart overcall your partner raises to two spades. As you are playing support doubles, her raise guarantees four trumps. She would have artificially doubled two hearts with only three spades. You are not surprised to hear your right-hand opponent raise to three hearts, confronting you with:

Partner	**RHO**	**You**	**LHO**
1 ◇	Pass	1 ♠	2 ♡
2 ♠ (4 cards)	3 ♡	??	

This one is easy. This one would probably be easy even without the LAW. In spite of your mere seven high-card points, this is a clear three-spade bid. What's this? With only eight trumps, we are competing on the three level?

For starters, we don't know how many hearts the opponents have. If they have nine or more, there

65

would be 17+ trumps and tricks, and either they or we will make our three-level contract. So, if they have 9+ hearts, we clearly want to bid. If they have only eight hearts (the worst-case scenario), then partner has four of them. Even if this is the case, there will still be 16 trumps, but probably more than 16 tricks.

The reason for the extra tricks comes from adjusting. All of our points are in our side's spade and diamond suits. Furthermore, there is a superb chance of a double fit. This deal just seems to have tons of tricks, and all lines of reasoning point towards a three-spade bid.

There were, in fact, 17 trumps and 18 tricks:

Dlr: North
Vul: Both

        ♠ K 8 7 2
        ♡ A 8 4
        ◇ K 9 5 3
        ♣ K 2

♠ J 10 6   ♠ 9 3
♡ K J 10 9 7   ♡ Q 5 3 2
◇ 8   ◇ A Q 6 2
♣ A Q J 10   ♣ 7 6 4

        ♠ A Q 5 4
        ♡ 6
        ◇ J 10 7 4
        ♣ 9 8 5 3

If you were teaching a friend the LAW, how would you discuss this full deal? We've already gone through the analysis of why South had a clear-cut three-spade bid. How many trumps are there? How many tricks are there?

There are 17 trumps, but you've noticed that there is an extra trick. Each side can make nine tricks. That's no surprise -- the deal is as pure as can be. All four suits pull their full weight on offense and defense. There are no "minor honors" anywhere. Although the deal is not a true double fit as we've defined it, (eight-plus in two suits for both sides), it's pretty close to being one. These factors combine to produce the extra trick. Remember, of course, that we had a strong indication of this extra trick just from looking at our hand and listening to the bidding.

As your experience at LAW reasoning grows, you'll find it very easy to lean in the right direction. On this deal you would be leaning towards extra tricks, and that would result in a three-spade call. When the adjustments have you leaning towards a lower number of tricks, you will often end up passing.

Here's a similar situation. Playing matchpoints with nobody vulnerable, you are in second seat holding:

♠ Q 10 x x ♡ x ◇ x x x x ♣ K x x x.

Your RHO opens one diamond, and after a one heart response, your partner makes a takeout double. Eventually you are confronted with this problem:

RHO	You	LHO	Partner
1◇	Pass	1♡	Dbl
2♡	2♠	3♡	Pass
Pass	??		

Does this seem like the old "eight-and-eight situation?" You have eight spades, and they might have only eight hearts. Does it mean that you should not bid "three-over-three?"

Not true at all! It's possible the trumps are "eight-and-eight," but then there would be 17 tricks.

Let's figure it out. Partner will typically have 4-4 in the black suits for his double, so we expect to have eight spades. If the opponents have eight hearts, then partner has four; so he is presumably 4-4-1-4. That makes the deal a double fitter. In addition to our spade suit, we have an eight-card club fit; the opponents also have an eight-card diamond fit besides their heart suit. Our adjustment guideline tells us to to add for the double fit.

68

Furthermore, if we thought about "minor honors" and purity, we might add another half or full trick. All of our points are in our suits, and we have nothing in their suits.

If partner doesn't have four hearts, then the total is 17 without any adjustments. They'll have nine hearts added to our eight spades.

All of this reasoning suggests that there should be at least 17 tricks, and that tells us to **bid**. One side will be making nine tricks for +140, so what good can come of passing?

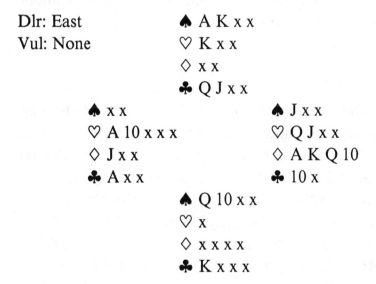

Dlr: East
Vul: None

♠ A K x x
♡ K x x
◇ x x
♣ Q J x x

♠ x x
♡ A 10 x x x
◇ J x x
♣ A x x

♠ J x x
♡ Q J x x
◇ A K Q 10
♣ 10 x

♠ Q 10 x x
♡ x
◇ x x x x
♣ K x x x

As you can see, both sides can take nine tricks. East-West lose two spades, a heart, and a club.

69

North-South lose two diamonds, a heart, and a club. As predicted, there were 17 trumps and 18 tricks.

Why the extra trick? Although there wasn't a true double fit, it appears that the extra trick results from the fact that all cards pulled their full weight.

Even the king of hearts, which is always a trick on defense, is also pulling its weight on offense. It's needed so that declarer can discard his fourth diamond. He can ruff only one diamond in dummy if the defenders lead trumps. And if they lead clubs, threatening a ruff, declarer must draw trumps himself. He will need to dispose of his fourth diamond on the heart king.

The 1992 Team Olympiad was held in Salsomaggiore, Italy, and might best be remembered for the stifling conditions. Temperatures near 100 degrees Fahrenheit had the players sweating profusely, as there was no air conditioning in the playing area! Naturally, what I usually remember about such tournaments are the LAW violations. In the finals, Hervè Mouïel, for the French team, held:

♠ 10 2 ♡ 10 9 8 4 ◊ J 6 2 ♣ A Q J 6.

With both sides vulnerable, he faced this decision:

South	West	North	East
Rodwell	Levy	Meckstroth	Mouïel
--	1 ◇	Pass	1 ♡
2 ♠	3 ◇	3 ♠	???

What would you do?

Mouïel chose to pass, and three spades became the final contract. Do you think he made a LAWful choice? Or an AWful choice?

His partner's free three-diamond bid had shown at least six, possibly seven diamonds. His opponents, for the jump overcall and raise, were quite likely to have nine spades. Mouïel should have figured on at least 18 trumps, enough to compete. The purity of his hand (the jack of his trump suit, no "minor honors" in spades) argued for at least 19 tricks and an even clearer reason to bid. Instead, he passed, and defended against three spades on this layout:

```
Dlr: West          ♠ J 9 4 3
Vul: Both          ♡ A Q 6
                   ◇ 10 8
                   ♣ 10 8 3 2
    ♠ A                      ♠ 10 2
    ♡ 7 2                    ♡ 10 9 8 4
    ◇ A K Q 7 4 3            ◇ J 6 2
    ♣ K 9 5 4                ♣ A Q J 6
                   ♠ K Q 8 7 6 5
                   ♡ K J 5 3
                   ◇ 9 5
                   ♣ 7
```

As you can see, three spades was an easy make, +140 for the Americans, while the French had 11 easy tricks available in diamonds! Notice that there were 19 trumps and 20 tricks. The extra trick comes from the extreme purity of the deal -- no wastage in any suit. East should have known to compete over three spades by considering the positive adjustment factors and how many trumps there rated to be. Instead, he made a LAW-breaking pass and received this citation.

See if you can use adjustments to solve this matchpoint problem. With nobody vulnerable, you hold this modest six count:

♠ Q J 9   ♡ x x   ◇ K x x x   ♣ x x x x.

Your partner opens one heart which is overcalled with one spade. You're a bit weak for a negative double, so you choose to pass. Your pesky LHO preempts to three spades (nobody gives you a free run these days), and your partner doubles for take-out. It's up to you:

Partner	RHO	You	LHO
1♡	1♠	Pass	3♠
Dbl	Pass	??	

This should be easy; the LAW was made for this kind of decision. Your partner is very likely to have one spade, five or six hearts, and three or four of each minor, 1-6-3-3, 1-5-4-3, or 1-5-3-4. If we were to bid four of a suit, on a good day there's a reasonable chance that we'd land in an eight-card fit. Adding that to the opponents' probable nine-card fit gives us at most 17 trumps. Our QJ9 of spades suggests a negative adjustment to maybe 16 or 16½ tricks. By now you might know without having to go through a "chart analysis" that there are not enough trumps to go to the four level! You're not likely to take 10 tricks -- and, if you do, they will be going down several in three spades doubled.

For a moment, let's also consider what the LAW says about bidding three notrump, assuming it's natural. The formula (from Chapter Seven of *To Bid or Not to Bid*) tells us to always add <u>seven</u> to the opponents' number of trumps. That would give us nine + <u>seven</u> or 16 total tricks if we were to play in notrump and they were to play in spades. If we have nine tricks for +400 in three notrump, then we should anticipate seven tricks for only +300 against three spades doubled. However, as this is the only case where bidding three notrump would be correct, it is better to pass. Furthermore, in three notrump, you expect that the defense will lead and clear spades, setting up four spade tricks. When you win your queen of spades, your side would need to run off the next eight tricks without losing the lead.

Here's a representative full deal:

```
Dlr: North          ♠ x
Vul: None           ♡ A K 9 x x
                    ◇ A 10 x x
                    ♣ A x x
         ♠ 10 x x x              ♠ A K x x x
         ♡ J 10 x x              ♡ Q x
         ◇ x x                   ◇ Q J x
         ♣ K 10 x                ♣ Q J x
                    ♠ Q J 9
                    ♡ x x
                    ◇ K x x x
                    ♣ x x x x
```

North	East	South	West
1♡	1♠	Pass	3♠
Dbl	Pass	??	

This is a most educational layout from a LAW point of view.

East-West have only seven tricks in spades, losing six obvious top tricks. North-South have only nine tricks in diamonds; with proper defense the opponents are entitled to a spade, a diamond, and two club tricks. There are 17 trumps, yet only 16 tricks.

During our LAW decision, we assumed 16½ tricks due to the minor spade honors. As it turned out, those "minor honors," in addition to East's in the diamond suit, caused the trick total to be one fewer than the number of trumps. No surprise!

So, you would pass three spades doubled with the South hand and score an excellent +300. But what happened to the poor West player who paid $12.95 for *To Bid or Not to Bid*? "Larry," he thinks, "you said that I'd be safe at the three level with nine trumps!"

He has a point. He could have bid only two spades and gone -110 by selling out to three diamonds. Minus 110 wouldn't be a very good score, but it would be better than -300! However, his three-spade bid will be a winner most of the time. In fact, if he wasn't playing against LAW abiding opponents, he would have survived on this deal. Perhaps some

North players would have chosen to pass the three spade bid, resulting in +100 to North-South, worse than +110 for making three diamonds. Of course, there are also LAWless South players who would pull the double, and thus, present East-West with a plus score.

Just in case West is still throwing the book at me, I'd like to point out the following alternative deal, a very typical type of layout where West's three-spade bid would meet with more success:

```
Dlr: North          ♠ Q x
Vul: None           ♡ K Q 9 x x
                    ◊ A 10 x x
                    ♣ A x
        ♠ 10 x x x              ♠ A K x x x
        ♡ J 10 x x              ♡ A x
        ◊ x x                   ◊ J x
        ♣ K 10 x                ♣ Q J x x
                    ♠ J 9
                    ♡ x x
                    ◊ K Q x x x
                    ♣ x x x x
```

North	East	South	West
1♡	1♠	Pass	3♠
Pass	Pass	??	

Now, West's three-spade bid would probably buy the contract for +140. A mere raise to two spades would allow North-South, especially if they were LAW-obeying, to find their diamond fit. If North-South were aware of the 18 trumps, they would compete to four diamonds over three spades. With each side having nine tricks, the best East-West could do would be +100 against four-diamonds doubled. West would be left wondering why he didn't bid three spades the first time.

Chapter 6 - Support with Support

Support with support. It sounds so simple, but it is so often ignored. My good friend Marty Bergen tries so hard to impose this elementary phrase on all of his students. In the classroom they seem to understand, but they mysteriously forget to bring their lessons to the table. When Marty and I play in the same event, we enjoy rehashing the deals. Recently, we were each playing with a student, and on three different deals from the same session, it was important to support with support.

Deal 1:

Dlr: North
Vul: None

```
                    ♠ 3
                    ♡ K 10 7 5
                    ◇ A J 10 7 6 5 4
                    ♣ 6
  ♠ Q 10 7 6                        ♠ A K J 8 4 2
  ♡ A Q 3                           ♡ 9 4 2
  ◇ 3                               ◇ 2
  ♣ A J 10 7 2                      ♣ 9 5 4
                    ♠ 9 5
                    ♡ J 8 6
                    ◇ K Q 9 8
                    ♣ K Q 8 3
```

North **Marty**	East	South **Student**	West
4 ◇	Pass	Pass	Dbl
Pass	4 ♠	ALL PASS	

79

Marty's student was afraid to raise to the five level. He could have been right -- maybe he'd go for -500 when the opponents were only entitled to +420. However, "supporting with support" is usually a good idea. In this case he should have expected 11 or 12 trumps, and thus, he should have bid to the five level. Five diamonds is down only one, and four spades makes easily. (Sure, a heart lead might beat it, but who would find that lead?)

Deal 2:

Dlr: North
Vul: E-W

```
                    ♠ 10 2
                    ♡ 9 8 7
                    ◇ K 10 8 4 2
                    ♣ A 10 2
    ♠ A J 6 4 3                 ♠ K 9 8 7 5
    ♡ K 5 4 3                   ♡ A 2
    ◇ Q 7                       ◇ J 5 3
    ♣ Q 3                       ♣ K 5 4
                    ♠ Q
                    ♡ Q J 10 6
                    ◇ A 9 6
                    ♣ J 9 8 7 6
```

North	East	South	West
Marty		**Student**	
2◇ !	Pass	Pass !!	2♠
Pass	4♠	ALL PASS	

80

What do you think of Marty's weak two-bid in diamonds? It's certainly not a classic, but for Marty it's routine. He loves to preempt, and at favorable vulnerability he has very low standards! His partner passed (he must be quite afraid of Marty's two-bids) and the opponents easily bid to four spades and scored 10 effortless tricks. Had Marty's student supported to three diamonds, East-West might never have entered the auction.

South should definitely boost the level of bidding and take away some of the opponents' exploratory space. Are you wondering about raising to the three level with only eight trumps? Opposite most players, you'd expect two diamonds to show six cards, so a raise to three would be indicated by the LAW (nine trumps). Even opposite a five-card suit (Marty's expected length), you should raise to three. Why?

Because of the total number of trumps! You have only one spade. You know that the opponents have at least eight and probably nine cards in that suit! So, there are at least 16 trumps/tricks giving you total safety in bidding three diamonds. If you are allowed to play there (you should be delighted), you will probably be -50 or -100, but you'll "know" that they can make at least +110 or +140 in spades. Don't expect that you might buy the contract in two diamonds. Support with support!

Raising to the three level with only eight trumps is often necessary. Your partner opens one diamond, RHO doubles, and you're looking at:

♠ x ♡ Q x x ◇ Q J x x ♣ x x x x x.

You can't count on partner for more than four diamonds, so your first LAW instinct should be to raise only to the eight-trump level -- two diamonds. However, since partner has at most four spades, you know the opponents have at least eight. Left to their own devices they'll surely compete to two spades. Accordingly, you should bid three diamonds. You're not going to let them play at the two level with eight trumps, so you might as well bid your hand to the limit immediately and make the preemptive jump. The "getting-past-the-opponents' LAW-level" theme occurs repeatedly. Try to get used to recognizing these situations. You open one club with:

♠ x ♡ A x x ◇ Q x x ♣ K Q J x x,

and your partner responds one notrump. RHO doubles, and it's your call. The "normal" action is two clubs, but don't you hate to make it so easy for them to locate their spade fit? Your partner has at most three spades for his one-notrump response, so the opponents have nine spades. I'd bid two notrump (Good-Bad - See Appendix B) to show a weak three-

82

level bid. Our partner must have at least three clubs (he didn't bid a suit), so the LAW clearly supports us at at least the three level!

Deal 3:

Dlr: East
Vul: N-S

```
                    ♠ K 10 7 5 3 2
                    ♡ J
                    ◇ A K 9 4
                    ♣ 6 2
   ♠ A 4                              ♠ J 8
   ♡ Q 5 3 2                          ♡ A K 10 8 6
   ◇ 10 5 3                           ◇ J 7 6
   ♣ A K 7 3                          ♣ J 10 5
                    ♠ Q 9 6
                    ♡ 9 7 4
                    ◇ Q 8 2
                    ♣ Q 9 8 4
```

North Marty	East	South Student	West
--	Pass	Pass	1♣
1♠	2♡	Pass	Pass
2♠	3♣	Pass	3♡
Pass	Pass	Pass	

Over which of South's passes did I want to place an exclamation point? Half of them.

The failure to raise to two spades is understandable. A flat six-count is a little bit less than partner might expect. You don't want him jumping to game. However, South clearly should have supported at either of his last two turns. Marty's bidding implied at least six spades -- look at that vulnerable two-spade rebid. North-South are known to have nine trumps, and accordingly, South should compete to the three level. Notice that three spades yields nine easy tricks, as does three hearts. Failure to support with support on this hand (nine trumps -- three level!!) gave North-South a very poor score.

What about my student? We were sitting the opposite direction, but I hope that if she were given a chance she would have correctly applied the LAW to get straight A's on all three problems.

Chapter 7 - Getting the LAW in the Game

You have to get in there! What would you do holding:

♠ A 8 6 ♡ A 9 7 ◇ 9 5 ♣ K J 9 7 4,

with nobody vulnerable after hearing the following:

RHO	You	LHO	Partner
1◇	Pass	1♡	Pass
1♠	Pass	2♠	Pass
Pass	??		

Does it matter if it's IMPS or matchpoints? Is it safe to balance with a three-club bid here? Partner might have:

♠ Q 2 ♡ J 8 6 5 4 ◇ Q 10 6 2 ♣ 6 5,

and we will go for a number. On the other hand, partner might have

♠ 7 5 ♡ Q 8 2 ◇ K 10 6 4 ♣ Q 10 5 3,

and everything will be fine. We might even push them to three spades, down one. How do we know?

This is a trick problem; you shouldn't ever get to

this position. Make a takeout double on the first round of the bidding! Get the hand off your chest. It's not a perfect takeout double, as you'd like to have four cards in at least one of the majors, but the alternative of passing often leads to much worse problems. You should strive not to overcall on the two-level with a so-so five-card suit, and thus, you can rule out a two-club bid.

It is relatively safe to make aggressive takeout doubles on the one level, especially if you're not vulnerable. Occasionally your LHO will have a great hand and redouble; eventually he'll double your side for a big penalty -- but I can't remember the last time that's happened. Who wants to defend against a doubled one-level contract?

Let's look at the possibility of "going for a number" in a one-level contract from a LAWyer's point of view. You can take the seat of the side trying to extract the penalty. Your partner opens one diamond, and the opponents make a takeout double, possibly of the frisky variety that I am recommending. You have some 4-3-3-3 twelve count and redouble with the hope that your side will subsequently be able to double and teach your opponents a sharp lesson. Invariably it goes one-of-a-suit on your left, pass - pass - back to you? Are you so anxious to double? Your partner won't have too many cards in their suit, or else he would have doubled. Who wants to defend a one-level contract when the opponents rate to have seven trumps and LAW protection?

Now, back to the aggressive takeout doublers. Because of the LAW protection, you can afford to be very aggressive with your one-level takeout doubles. The opponents simply won't be anxious to penalize you, and even if they do, you should be okay with your seven trumps on the one level.

All that is necessary is for your partner to be aware that your takeout doubles might be a point or two lighter than "standard" and respond accordingly. You'll find that you and your partner are able to get into many more auctions at low and safe levels -- which is what competitive bidding is all about. Your opponents will not be pleased to hear you in their auctions so often.

One little adjunct to this aggressive philosophy is some of the agreements you and your partner should have after your takeout double is redoubled. First, it is important for good partnerships to have an agreement as to what a pass shows. For example,

Opener	You	Responder	Partner
1 ◊	Dbl	Rdbl	*Pass*

Does the pass mean that your partner wants to defend one diamond redoubled? It's possible to play it that way, but not very practical. Most experts play that the pass in this position shows a hand with nothing special to say. It basically says, "you got us in, you get us out." A typical hand might be:

♠ x x x ♡ x x x ◇ x x x x ♣ A x x.

What suit would you want to bid after hearing the redouble?

Taking out the double shouldn't promise values. For example, after:

LHO	Partner	RHO	You
1 ◇	Dbl	Rdbl	??

wouldn't you have to bid one heart with as little as:

♠ x x ♡ x x x x ◇ x x x x x ♣ x x?

You couldn't pass with that hand, since the takeout doubler might hold:

♠ K x x x ♡ A x x ◇ x x ♣ A Q x x.

Your one-heart bid probably won't be doubled, and at least your side will be in its seven-card fit. If you pass one-diamond redoubled around to partner, he would run to one spade, and your side would be in big trouble.

Once you have an understanding as to what one-level responses and passes of the redouble show, you can go on to make agreements about jumps. What I (and the LAW) suggest is that jumps after a one-level takeout double is redoubled should be played as weak! For example, you hold:

♠ Q J 9 5 3   ♡ 8 6   ◇ 7 4 2   ♣ 6 3 2,

and partner doubles their one-diamond opening; RHO redoubles. Sure, you could bid a safe one spade, but two spades, weak, is much more delight-ful, as well as LAW protected. It's almost impossible that you will have a strong hand and need two spades as value showing. LHO has an opening bid, partner has made a takeout double, and RHO has 10+. What does that leave for us? Even if you do happen to have values, it's very unlikely your side has a game. If you really want to show strength, you can make a minimum bid and then bid again later -- surely the auction won't die.

The weak jump-response after the redouble is a useful and most effective bid which occurs frequently at the table. Let's put the above:

♠ Q J 9 5 3   ♡ 8 6   ◇ 7 4 2   ♣ 6 3 2

opposite our aggressive takeout double:

♠ A 8 6   ♡ A 9 7   ◇ 9 5   ♣ K J 9 7 4,

in this full deal:

```
Dlr: West              ♠ A 8 6
Vul: None              ♡ A 9 7
                       ◇ 9 5
                       ♣ K J 9 7 4
        ♠ 10 7 2                   ♠ K 4
        ♡ K J 10 2                 ♡ Q 8 5 3
        ◇ A Q 8 3                  ◇ K J 10 6
        ♣ A 8                      ♣ Q 10 5
                       ♠ Q J 9 5 3
                       ♡ 6 4
                       ◇ 7 4 2
                       ♣ 6 3 2
```

West	North	East	South
1◇	Dbl	Rdbl	2♠
Pass	Pass	??	

My guess is that East would bid two notrump, raised by West to three notrump, down one after your spade lead. In a duplicate game, the other East-West's, who haven't had any obstructive bids by North-South, will have a much easier time. They, no doubt, will reach the laydown four hearts.

After an opponent's redouble, a jump to the three level is also preemptive. It simply shows more shape (trumps) than a two-level jump. After

LHO	**Partner**	**RHO**	**You**
1 ◇	Dbl	Rdbl	??

I would jump preemptively to three spades with:

♠ J 10 x x x x   ♡ x x x   ◇ x x   ♣ x x.

In fact, it is "standard" to play this double jump as weak even without the redouble. Of course, a single jump response to a takeout double (no redouble) is intermediate, a hand with about 8-11 points.

When your partner makes a takeout double, and you know your side has lots of trumps, make sure you skip the bidding. You'll have a lot more fun preempting -- being a pain in the neck for your opponents -- than you will passing -- watching them bid unbothered to consistently good contracts.

You can use the LAW as your protective crutch to constantly be an annoying opponent. (You can be a lovely person, nice, polite, smiling -- but don't sit there passing!) Get in and let your partner jump to a safe LAW level, or let your partner get in, and you do the obstructing.

Chapter 8 - Legal Stealing

On only one-fourth of bridge deals does one side have 26 or more high-card points. On some of those 25% the other side can get their money's worth by preempting, but on most occasions they'll just have to sit there and pass, praying that their opponents' constructive bidding isn't very good.

On three-fourths of bridge deals, neither side will have as many as 26 high-card points. When the points are split 20-20, 19-21, or 18-22 (these three groups encompass 40% of all deals), the LAW of Total Tricks will almost always come into play. Both sides are likely to be in the auction, with the LAW governing the competitive battle. Even when the points are split 17-23, 16-24, and 15-25, the LAW is lurking in the background.

There is a small school of bridge theorists (most notably Al Roth and Matthew & Pam Granovetter) who advocate sound opening bids, coupled with a sound bidding system. They believe that it is easier to bid constructively if your partner knows that you have full opening values. If you'd like to learn more about their theories, I suggest that you read a book on the Roth-Stone bidding system.

I don't advocate a sound structure, and the majority of players today concur. An aggressive style isn't much of a hindrance to our own constructive bidding. Where we particularly have an advantage is in the competitive auctions -- most bridge deals. What we are engaged in is often an attempt to *steal*.

Most bridge deals have at least 14 tricks. After all, each side always has at least seven trumps. By getting into the auction early, and bidding at the one or two level, you are only contracting for seven or eight tricks. If you go down, the opponents will surely have a contract their way. If you open one spade with:

♠ K J 9 x x ♡ A x ◇ K x x ♣ x x x,

the Roth-Stoner's will call you crazy. I'll call you a winner. Your partner raises to two spades with his

♠ Q x x ♡ x x x ◇ A x x x ♣ J 10 x.

Will you make two spades? No, you'll probably lose a spade, a heart, a diamond, and three clubs, resulting in down one. But what's wrong with that? The opponents have an eight-card heart fit. Let's see what they can make.

They presumably have nine tricks available in hearts -- and will lose at most a spade, a heart, and two diamond tricks. You're not surprised. There are 16 trumps, and as your side has only seven tricks, why shouldn't they have nine?

So this is what I'm trying to say. Get in there and bid to your heart's content (or any other suit for that matter!). Agree with your partner to open light, respond light, and get to where you're going before the opponents can properly exchange information of their own.

All of the sound-initial-action advocates rant and rave about the good constructive auctions they have. They seem to forget how easy they make things for their opponents. It's so easy to play against sound bidders -- you never seem to be under any pressure. Alternatively, it is everyone's worst nightmare to play against an active pair such as Meckstroth-Rodwell. Those bandits are in there bidding on nothing on every hand. It's a royal pain to play against them. No wonder that they are widely regarded as the best pair in the world!

Once you agree to "bid on nothing," you can familiarize yourself with other ways to steal and obstruct. Try to exercise a little caution when vulnerable, and always use the idea of LAW protection as your safety net.

At favorable vulnerability your partner opens one heart and you hold:

♠ x x ♡ 10 9 x ◇ J x x x ♣ Q x x x.

Your right-hand opponent passes. The "book" tells you to pass, but sometimes the "book" needs rewriting.

Perhaps you're familiar with one notrump forcing; many good players would use it with this hand. Even if it's not forcing, one notrump is a very good tactical response. There are a few unfortunate things that could happen; for example, partner could jump to three notrump or a new suit, or partner could double them, expecting you to have something. However, the potential rewards from bidding one notrump far outweigh those few bad possibilities. Your partner will alert your one-notrump response, and say that it shows "up to 12 points."

Your left-hand opponent no doubt has a good hand, and your right-hand opponent probably isn't broke. When you respond one notrump, they will have a hard time realizing that the hand belongs to them. Additionally, your side will have full LAW protection if you eventually bid to two hearts, and you'll even be okay if your partner makes a jump rebid to three hearts. He'll go down, no doubt, but you can rest assured that with your side holding nine trumps, your score of -50 or -100 will be well compensated by a scoresheet full of 110's or 140's the other way!

Here is an example of how this undervalued one notrump can work out:

Dlr: North
Vul: E-W

```
                  ♠ A 9 x
                  ♡ K Q J x x
                  ◇ K 10 x x
                  ♣ x
  ♠ Q 10 x x x               ♠ K J x
  ♡ x x                      ♡ A x x
  ◇ A 9 x                    ◇ Q x
  ♣ A J 10                   ♣ K 9 x x x
                  ♠ x x
                  ♡ 10 9 x
                  ◇ J x x x
                  ♣ Q x x x
```

North	East	South	West
1♡	Pass	1NT	Pass
2◇	Pass	2♡	ALL PASS

Would you enter the bidding, vulnerable, with the East-West cards? It's quite dangerous to do so. Although best defense will beat it, North-South might make two hearts. Meantime, East-West do

97

very well in spades, probably 10 tricks for +170 or maybe even +620. If South passes the one-heart opening, West has a very easy one-spade bid, and East-West will end up in a spade partscore or game.

This "stealing" can be lots of fun for your side, so, since the LAW will protect you, why not give it a try?

Chapter 9 - Dutch LAW

Outstanding hospitality. Exceptional playing conditions. Extraordinary publicity. Enormous crowds of spectators around every table. A phenomenal field of 16 of the world's best pairs. Long-standing partnerships such as Meckstroth-Rodwell, Chagas-Branco and Hamman-Wolff. International stars such as France's Paul Chemla and Pakistan's Zia Mahmood. Every round a battle of titans.

Cap Volmac (part of the Cap Gemini Sogeti Group), a computer software company, sponsors an incredible bridge competition. The tournament, which grows in stature every year, is considered to be simply the best bridge tournament on our planet.

The 1994 edition was held in January in The Hague, and needless to say, the partisan viewgraph audience was rooting hard for the three newly crowned Dutch World Champion pairs. However, the event was won by Norwegians Tor Helness and Geir Helgemo. At 23, Helgemo became the youngest winner ever of this prestigious tournament.

Over the course of the four-day tournament, there were numerous LAW of Total Tricks decisions to be made. It still amazes me how some of the world's very best players continually violate the LAW.

Hervé Mouïel of France has won more world championships than most of us, and I trust he will take my criticism with good humor. On the first board of our match against him, he held:

♠ K 8 6 ♡ 10 8 7 4 ◇ A 10 ♣ A J 8 3.

With nobody vulnerable he sat in fourth seat, IMP scoring. My partner, David Berkowitz, opened with one heart, and Mouïel's partner, Alain Levy, over-called one spade. Mouïel redoubled my negative double, and David bid two clubs, which was passed around to Mouïel. He cuebid two hearts and his partner bid two spades. I now competed to three clubs and it was up to him:

Berkowitz	Levy	Cohen	Mouïel
1♡	1♠	Dbl	Rdbl
2♣	Pass	Pass	2♡
Pass	2♠	3♣	??

You, no doubt, recognize this as a classic "eight-and-eight" situation. You can almost bet on the fact that both sides have eight trumps. Unless there are lots of positive adjustment factors, you should never outbid your opponents on the three level with 16 trumps. Instead of passing, you might choose to double, especially if scoring was by matchpoints.

How many tricks do you expect? Sixteen you say. Probably right, but you might decide, due to adjustments, that there is a good chance for only 15 tricks. The jack of clubs is a big warning (a "minor honor") to adjust downwards and expect fewer tricks than trumps. With 15 or even 16 tricks, why would you ever contract for nine tricks when your opponents have already done so?

Mouïel chose to bid three spades, and everyone passed. I led a heart, saw the dummy, and knew that I had material to write about. I regret that after the match I didn't ask Mr. Mouïel what his logic was for bidding three spades. I suspect he mentally placed his partner with a singleton club and therefore, decided that the hands "fit" well. This is the most common type of error made by players of all levels. They have four cards in the opponents' suit, expect a singleton opposite, and think that this set-up bodes well for declaring the hand.

Bad thinking. Holding four cards in the opponents' suit should send one loud and clear message: DEFEND!

Dlr: South   ♠ A 9 7
Vul: None   ♡ 9 2
                ◊ K Q 9 8
                ♣ 10 9 5 2

♠ J 10 5 4 2   ♠ K 8 6
♡ A J   ♡ 10 8 7 4
◊ 7 6 5 3 2   ◊ A 10
♣ 4   ♣ A J 8 3

                ♠ Q 3
                ♡ K Q 6 5 3
                ◊ J 4
                ♣ K Q 7 6

South Berkowitz	West Levy	North Cohen	East Mouïel
1♡	1♠	Dbl	Rdbl
2♣	Pass	Pass	2♡
Pass	2♠	3♣	3♠!
ALL PASS			

Personally, I would have shown a good spade raise
on the first round of bidding with the East hand.
The deal is a bit complex, but the main theme that
comes lucidly through is that there are not enough
trumps! For example, consider North-South playing
in three clubs. After a spade lead, they'll lose a trick
in each side suit. What about the trumps? They
can't be handled easily. Yes, double-dummy the suit
can be picked up by taking a deep finesse for the

eight, but who would do that? Furthermore, even if the club suit could be "played in a vacuum," the rest of the deal is just too difficult to handle. There are red-suit losers to worry about, communication problems, etc. Three clubs was not made at any table.

What about three spades? Troubles of the same kind. Not enough trumps. What can East-West do about the diamond losers? Trump them in dummy? They can't be dealt with. Levy won the heart lead and chose to play a trump to the *king* and a trump back. Dummy's heart spots proved useful, but Levy simply could not avoid the loss of two trump tricks, one heart, one diamond, and a trick "in the wash." He could not dispose of all of his diamond losers. I'll say it one more time . . . not enough trumps.

Later in the match Mouïel again violated the LAW, this time so badly that I can only guess that he had something tactical in mind. Holding:

♠ 10 5 ♡ 8 5 4 2 ◇ J 10 8 7 3 ♣ J 5,

at favorable vulnerability, his partner opened one spade, and the auction proceeded:

Berkowitz	Levy	Cohen	Mouïel
--	1♠	Dbl	Pass
1NT	2◇	3♣	??

103

Perhaps you think this is silly. It doesn't take a LAW degree to know that you have nine or more trumps, and thus can safely bid at the three level, in spite of your two high-card points. Wouldn't most players think it automatic to bid three diamonds here? For reasons unknown to you and me, Mouïel "jumped to pass" (my derogatory way of describing an inexplicable underbid), and this was the full deal:

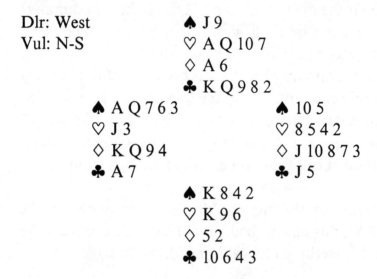

```
Dlr: West        ♠ J 9
Vul: N-S         ♡ A Q 10 7
                 ◇ A 6
                 ♣ K Q 9 8 2
    ♠ A Q 7 6 3           ♠ 10 5
    ♡ J 3                 ♡ 8 5 4 2
    ◇ K Q 9 4             ◇ J 10 8 7 3
    ♣ A 7                 ♣ J 5
                 ♠ K 8 4 2
                 ♡ K 9 6
                 ◇ 5 2
                 ♣ 10 6 4 3
```

Both sides have nine trumps and nine tricks. East-West lose two hearts, a club, and the trump ace. North-South lose two spades, a diamond, and only the ace of trumps. The jack of clubs almost plays a role as a "minor honor," but best play by declarer will prevent it from taking a trick. Why Mouïel chose to pass remains a mystery to me, but I'd be remiss if I didn't point out that he and Levy finished a very respectable third place in the event. Perhaps these were his only two LAW violations of the tournament.

In round one of the event, I would have done well to follow my own advice. What would you do if your partner passed, and Bob Hamman opened four hearts on your right? I was at favorable vulnerability holding:

♠ K J 10 9 5 ♡ 4 ◇ A Q J ♣ K 10 6 5.

One of the curious things about the LAW is that bidding "four spades over four hearts" is one of the most rewarding practices in bridge. Without having read Chapter Eight of *To Bid or Not to Bid*, you might find it hard to see what this has to do with the LAW, but I'll try to briefly explain.

If there are 18 trumps, which is very often the case when trying to decide what to do on the four level, you would normally choose to defend. This is because both contracts are often going down. Why should you bid four diamonds over four clubs if there are 18 trumps/tricks? If both sides have nine tricks, neither will make its contract. If one side has 10 and the other eight, there's no good reason to play the hand. It's the same reasoning we use for not bidding "three-over-three" with 16 trumps. The scoring table simply does not reward such an action.

However, everything changes when the decision is four spades over four hearts. Now, with 18 tricks divided 10 and eight, there is every reason to play the hand. If your side has the 10 tricks, you'll get the additional game bonus and thus, score much better than defending. If their side has the 10 tricks, you'll want to sacrifice in four spades. If the tricks are split nine and nine, you're only turning a very small plus into a very small minus. This is one further reason why I objected to Mr. Kaplan's "illegal" comment on page 52.

When there are 19 trumps, it is even more clear to bid four spades over four hearts. Even if there are only 17 trumps, bidding four spades will often show a profit, especially at favorable vulnerability. That is why I recommend . . .

> **When in doubt, bid four spades over four hearts.**

This rule is even more applicable over a four-heart *opening bid*. This is because the opener will often have an eight-card suit, producing extra tricks. It is a significant positive adjustment factor, which often results in one or two more tricks than trumps.

So, stupid me, when I held the above hand against Hamman, I ignored my own advice and chose to double. Everyone passed, and I guessed to lead a trump. This was the full deal:

```
Dlr: North        ♠ 8 7
Vul: E-W          ♡ A 10 7
                  ◇ K 10 4 2
                  ♣ J 9 4 2
     ♠ A 6 4 3 2              ♠ Q
     ♡ 3                      ♡ K Q J 9 8 6 5 2
     ◇ 9 8 7 6 5              ◇ 3
     ♣ A 7                    ♣ Q 8 3
                  ♠ K J 10 9 5
                  ♡ 4
                  ◇ A Q J
                  ♣ K 10 6 5
```

North	East	South	West
Berkowitz	Hamman	Cohen	Wolff
Pass	4♡	Dbl	Pass
Pass	Pass		

When I first saw the dummy, I was glad I had decided not to bid four spades. However, the play in four spades actually works quite well. At all tables where four spades was the contract, declarer won the heart lead, played a spade to the queen and king, ducked by West. West also ducked the next spade, which allowed declarer to get to dummy. Next, the jack of clubs was led, and passed around to West's ace. Declarer would then win any return and finish drawing the trumps. Then a diamond was led to dummy to repeat the club finesse. The defense took only the two black aces and declarer made five! (Please indulge my brief diversion into a description of the play of the hand -- we don't have to talk about bidding on every page!)

I'd like to point out that West's instinctive play of ducking the second spade was quite an error. If he had won the second round of trumps, he could have deprived declarer of a key entry to dummy. He could throw declarer back into his hand; South would draw trumps, and then face a serious dilemma in this position:

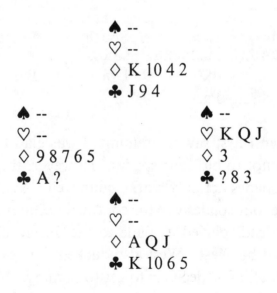

Declarer needs five more tricks for his contract. Four diamond tricks are easy, but what about the clubs? Declarer must assume that the ace is with West, or he has no chance. In the diagram, the ace is accordingly shown in the West hand. The question marks indicate that declarer doesn't know who has the queen of clubs.

If West has it, declarer will fail in his contract if he cashes three rounds of diamonds. He would be creating the setting trick for the defense via the fifth round of diamonds. (West wins the queen of clubs, and drives out the fourth diamond.)

On the other hand, if declarer crosses in diamonds and takes a club play, he will fail if East has the club queen. West would win the ace of clubs and exit with a diamond, locking declarer in his hand. Declarer never gets the fourth diamond winner and has to let East in with the queen of clubs.

Declarer could make the hand if he guesses how to do it, but it's far from obvious. He has to cash three (or four) rounds of diamonds, and then play East for the club queen.

The play in four hearts doubled was also exciting, but the best defense will always hold declarer to his nine top winners. Don't think that I enjoyed watching Hamman run his hearts, causing me to sweat on every trick. In the ending I had to throw my ace of diamonds to avoid being endplayed, and we were +200, but still a bad result since the field was making four spades doubled our way. Next time, I'm bidding four spades myself!

The Cap Volmac tournament is just one of many special bridge events that takes place in Holland. The Dutch take their bridge quite seriously. To prepare for the 1993 World Championships, they held a series of practice matches near a town called Vorden, at the castle of Hans Melchers. The setting was more pristine and elegant than could possibly be imagined.

Tables with screens and bidding boxes were brought in. Eric Kokish was hired as a coach for the Dutch team, and he spent many months working on systems with the players. Mr. Melchers flew in expert pairs from other countries in order to get the best possible practice for Holland's team.

My partner, David Berkowitz, and I, along with several other Americans, were invited to the castle in April 1993. We played 160 deals, and our American team proved to be ungracious guests as we defeated the Dutch team by a significant margin. Did they learn anything from the practice? I would say so. Later that year they faced our team in Santiago, Chile. Both of us had made it all the way to the semifinals of the Bermuda Bowl. However, this time it was the Dutch who were victorious. After dispatching our team by 3 IMPS, they went on to beat Norway for the world title. Practice makes perfect!

Do you think that one of their star players, Henri Leufkens, learned from this deal in the castle? With both sides vulnerable, he held:

♠ Q 8 ♡ K 9 8 4 2 ◊ J 6 ♣ A K 6 2.

He chose to bid three hearts in this auction:

Cohen	Westra	Berkowitz	Leufkens
1♠	Pass	1NT*	Pass
2♣	Pass	3♣	3♡
ALL PASS			

* Semi-forcing (opener passes with a balanced minimum)

Leufkens probably thought something along the lines of, "My partner must have only one club, and thus some heart length, so hearts should play well . . ."

What do you as a LAW person think of the three-heart bid? You'd think that the opponents probably have eight clubs, so your partner probably has only one. Partner has at least four spades or else the opponents would have agreed on spades, not clubs.

111

What about partner's diamond and heart length? Who knows? He might have four of each (4-4-4-1). He could be 5-2-5-1, or more optimistically 5-4-3-1. If you had to guess, he's likely to have more diamonds and fewer hearts, since you have only two diamonds and the opponents don't seem to have too many of that suit.

The bottom line is that by bidding three hearts, you're hoping that partner has four hearts, giving your side nine. Even if he has four hearts, your hand screams for negative adjustments. Your king of clubs is clearly huge on defense, but may prove worthless in hearts (it might provide a useless discard). Furthermore, even if you have nine trumps and no negative adjustments, your three-heart contract would yield +140 if it makes instead of the +100 you'd receive for beating three clubs (eight tricks). At IMP scoring, this would only be a 1-IMP swing.

Reading the above analysis may have been quite tedious, as it's full of theory and suppositions. But, is there any of it that doesn't make sense? This kind of reasoning is essential to making good LAW decisions and thus, good competitive bidding decisions. You, no doubt, would have judged to pass three clubs, and this would be your reward:

Dlr: West
Vul: Both

```
                    ♠ K 9 6 5 2
                    ♡ 10 6 5
                    ◇ Q 10 9 7
                    ♣ 3
    ♠ A 10 7 4 3                    ♠ J
    ♡ Q 7                           ♡ A J 3
    ◇ A K                           ◇ 8 5 4 3 2
    ♣ 10 9 8 5                      ♣ Q J 7 4
                    ♠ Q 8
                    ♡ K 9 8 4 2
                    ◇ J 6
                    ♣ A K 6 2
```

Leufkens was defeated two tricks in three hearts, for a score of -200. The defense took two high diamonds, ace of spades and a ruff, and then led another diamond, guaranteeing two additional trump tricks. At the other table three clubs was defeated one trick. At some point the defense played three rounds of trumps, and declarer was a trick short. This deal contained 16 trumps, but only 15 tricks. Not a surprise, with all the "minor honors." The LAW violation cost the Dutch team 7 IMPS.

Several months later in Chile, the Dutch were making much better total-tricks decisions. Kokish had done a lot of work with them. He spent endless hours in the castle teaching the team how to use the LAW in competitive auctions.

In Santiago, playing against Holland, I remember holding this hand:

♠ K x ♡ K x x ◇ x x x ♣ A K x x.

With nobody vulnerable, the bidding began one spade on my right. I chose to make a takeout double, and LHO raised to two spades. My partner, holding 3-5-2-3 distribution, bid three hearts. RHO passed, I passed, and LHO passed. The full deal is irrelevant here. What's important is that the Dutch knew to let us have it on the three level in this typical eight-and-eight situation. I remember thinking, "These guys are now well-trained." I would have much preferred to defend three spades than to play in three hearts. In fact, each side had eight tricks. When your opponents know the LAW, it makes it much more difficult to win!

While we're on the Holland subject, here's one other relevant hand from the practice match in April. With both sides vulnerable you hold:

♠ J 4 2 ♡ Q 10 6 5 ◇ 10 8 6 ♣ 5 4 3.

Your LHO opens one spade, and your partner bids two spades, showing hearts and a minor. This is doubled by your RHO.

LHO	Partner	RHO	You
1♠	2♠	Dbl	??

You think to yourself, "Since we have nine hearts, bidding three hearts seems perfect." Or do you? Let's think a bit more. Our partner has at least five hearts and at least five cards in a minor. In the other suits he is at most 2-1. That means that the opponents have at least eight spades, and at least eight of the minor that we don't have.

We also have two fits of at least eight cards. This is definitely a double fit, and we know to adjust by adding a trick. Furthermore, there is an excellent chance for purity. If partner has no spade honor, we can see that the deal might be pure. We have nothing wasted in their suits.

Now let's estimate the total trick count. We have nine or more trumps. The opponents have at least nine trumps in one of their suits (the one in which partner has a singleton). There are at least 18 trumps, and after our positive adjustments, there are 19 or 20 tricks. Thus we conclude it would be a big "total-tricks" underbid to respond only three hearts. Four hearts would be my choice, but even five hearts is a plausible bid. This was the full deal:

```
Dlr: South              ♠ 6
Vul: Both               ♡ A K J 9 7
                        ◇ A Q 7 4 2
                        ♣ 9 7
        ♠ K 9 8 7 5 3              ♠ A Q 10
        ♡ 2                        ♡ 8 4 3
        ◇ --                       ◇ K J 9 5 3
        ♣ K Q J 10 8 2             ♣ A 6
                        ♠ J 4 2
                        ♡ Q 10 6 5
                        ◇ 10 8 6
                        ♣ 5 4 3
```

A very unusual West hand . . . but that does not
take away from the question of South's proper LAW
bid. Obviously, the more hearts he bids, the harder
it will be for the opponents to reach their cold slam.
South must appreciate that his flat three-count is
definitely worth a jump if he brings the LAW into play.

Chapter 10 - U.S. LAW

"Larry, I've been using the LAW at our club and it's really helping." This from my cousin Susie in Memphis. She's helped me with my bridge-writing endeavors (someone has to fix my grammar) and she gets a first-hand look at all of the LAW material. "I held five spades to the king-jack-ten, three clubs to the ten, the jack-ten and another diamond, and king and one heart." Pretty good, I think -- she only learned bridge a few years ago. More advanced players than she often give me hands with only 12 cards in them! Far be it for me to complain that she hasn't given me spades, hearts, diamonds and clubs in that order.

"My RHO opened one spade, and I passed. It went one notrump on my left, and my partner doubled." She finished giving me the auction, and presented this problem:

♠ K J 10 7 2   ♡ K 5   ◇ J 10 7   ♣ 10 4 3

RHO	My Cousin	LHO	Her Partner
1♠	Pass	1NT	Dbl
2♡	Pass	3◇	Pass
Pass	??		

I believe that 99 out of 100 players would pass. Not my cousin. She reasoned as follows: "Partner must have length in all suits except spades for the takeout double. Because of that, the opponents rate to have no more than seven diamonds. The hand is a misfit (negative adjustment factor). The KJ10xx of spades ("minor honors" in their suit) are offside and lying very badly for declarer. The J10x of diamonds are probably of value on defense against a diamond contract -- especially if partner has some holding like Kxx. Our side has at least half the deck (partner's double shows opening-bid strength). They can't have many trumps (partner has at least two, probably three diamonds)." She concluded that there weren't enough trumps to let the opponents take nine tricks, and doubled. Quite a courageous action, but the winning one:

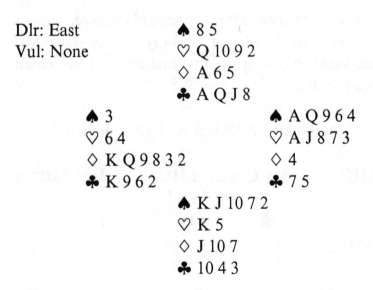

```
Dlr: East          ♠ 8 5
Vul: None          ♡ Q 10 9 2
                   ◇ A 6 5
                   ♣ A Q J 8
      ♠ 3                      ♠ A Q 9 6 4
      ♡ 6 4                    ♡ A J 8 7 3
      ◇ K Q 9 8 3 2            ◇ 4
      ♣ K 9 6 2                ♣ 7 5
                   ♠ K J 10 7 2
                   ♡ K 5
                   ◇ J 10 7
                   ♣ 10 4 3
```

The declarer lost six tricks and was -300. The play is quite complicated to analyze, but a quick glance shows that three-diamonds doubled is not a happy contract. At most other tables the hand was played by East-West and they were -50, -100, -150, etc. The really good scores went to the North-South pairs who realized that there was a shortage of total trumps/tricks and backed this logic by making a penalty double.

Playing with a friend in the 1993 Darien, Connecticut sectional, I witnessed one of the most unusual dummies of my career. My hand was an innocent looking:

♠ A J 7 4 3 ♡ 4 ♢ K 10 5 2 ♣ J 6 4.

Vulnerable against not, my partner opened the bidding with one heart. I responded one spade, and my LHO overcalled with one notrump. This was natural and strong (16-18); I can't say enough bad things about this treatment. To avoid offending anyone, I'll simply say that this bid is better played as a shaped light takeout.

My partner, an inexperienced player, passed. (Is that a clue as to which hand was the amazing dummy?) Two spades on my right was alerted as a transfer to clubs. Doubling a transfer normally asks for a lead in the artificial suit, but here it seemed that it should simply show extra values. As much as I hated to give the opponents extra room in this kind of auction, I decided to venture a double. Sure enough, my LHO bid three clubs, which was alerted as promising at least three clubs.

A nice little agreement to have. I suggest that you discuss with your partner what various actions mean after your transfer bid has been doubled. The most common cases are:

Opener		**Responder**	
1NT	Pass	2♢	Dbl

or

Opener		**Responder**	
1NT	Pass	2♡	Dbl

When the opponents double these transfers for the lead, the one-notrump bidder has three choices. He can pass, redouble, or accept the transfer. A redouble is an attempt to play the contract right there in the artificial suit! Pass is available as an extra call, and I suggest you define it to show exactly two cards in partner's suit. Accepting the transfer should promise three-card support. (With four I suggest bidding to the three level as discussed in Chapter Four of *To Bid or Not to Bid.*)

Back to our auction, where the three-club bid is followed by two passes, leaving it up to me:

Inexperienced Partner	RHO	Me	LHO
1♡	Pass	1♠	1NT
Pass	2♠*	Dbl	3♣**
Pass	Pass	??	

♠ A J 7 4 3	
♡ 4	* Transfer to clubs
◊ K 10 5 2	** Promising at least three clubs
♣ J 6 4	

The two-spade bidder presumably has a six-card club suit. With five, she would normally have passed one notrump. Based on this assumption, the opponents have nine clubs, so they are quite content on the three level.

If they have nine clubs, we must have at least an eight-card fit somewhere. Why is that?

There are only 26 cards in the combined hands of our partnership. Since they have nine clubs, we have only four. That leaves 22 slots free for the other three suits. If we hold seven cards in each of the other suits, there would still be an empty slot. One of those suits must have an eighth card.

If we have eight trumps and they have nine, somebody will be able to make nine tricks. Obviously, if we're making nine tricks, we want to bid to the three level, and even if they're making nine, we don't want to be -110.

And so, I bid three diamonds. If my partner had four of those, he'd pass. With fewer than four, something like 3-6-3-1, I assumed he would show preference for spades. If he were 2-7-3-1, he could bid three hearts. With both of these patterns he might have bid after the one-notrump overcall, but as I said before, this was not an experienced player.

My three-diamond call elicited an unusual response from partner -- he jumped to five diamonds! The one-notrump overcaller gleefully doubled, and I wondered how I was going to manage to take 11 tricks.

Talk about getting punished for balancing! Did my partner find an ace? Is there really a hand that could make all of those passes and then, all of a sudden, jump to five diamonds?

After the opening lead was made, I jokingly said "Sounds like you're 6-6 or something!" I hope the opponents didn't think I had a wire on the board, for this was the full deal:

```
Dlr: North          ♠ 9
Vul: N-S            ♡ A 9 8 7 6 5
                    ◇ Q 8 7 6 4 3
                    ♣ --
        ♠ K Q 10 8                  ♠ 6 5 2
        ♡ K Q J 3                   ♡ 10 2
        ◇ A                         ◇ J 9
        ♣ K Q 7 2                   ♣ A 10 9 8 5 3
                    ♠ A J 7 4 3
                    ♡ 4
                    ◇ K 10 5 2
                    ♣ J 6 4
```

North	East	South	West
1 ♡	Pass	1 ♠	1NT
Pass	2 ♠ *	Dbl	3 ♣ **
Pass	Pass	3 ◇	Pass
5 ◇	Pass	Pass	Dbl
ALL PASS			

* Transfer to clubs
** Promising at least three clubs

The dummy hit with a thud. I love it when partner has lots of trumps for me, but this was really a bonanza!

123

No doubt you agree with my three-diamond bid -- the LAW validated it. But, what do you think about everyone else's bidding?

East was perfect.

Unfortunately, West and North were not. I don't really like the one-heart opening, but if I deemed the hand worth an opening bid, I would surely follow up by bidding two diamonds on the next round. Already I've expressed my opinion of West's natural one notrump; the fact that it was off-shape and over-strength just makes me hate it more. Over my double, West probably should have bid four clubs. Not only does it look right on values, but nothing bad ever happened to anyone who bid to the four level with 10 trumps. In this case it would have probably kept our diamond fit hidden forever.

Looking at all four hands, no doubt you can see a way that I could have taken twelve tricks. In practice, I did a lot of cross-ruffing, and eventually lost a trick to East's jack of diamonds for +750 (making five) and a tie for top.

It's a silly deal, but I can't sleep at night until I see how many total tricks and trumps there are. There were 10 diamonds and 10 clubs for a total of 20 trumps. They can be held to 10 tricks in clubs (off two aces and a heart ruff). We took eleven (I know, a better declarer might have taken 12) for a total of 21 tricks. The extra trick or two results from the wild shape. If you look at the chart of adjustments on page 43, you will see that extreme distribution (Positive Shape) is a factor that will usually result in more tricks than trumps.

Playing against weak opponents in your local duplicate, you deal as South and open one diamond holding:

♠ Q J x ♡ A x x x ◇ A Q J x x ♣ x.

With nobody vulnerable, West doubles, and you are eventually confronted with a four-level decision:

West	North	East	South
--	--	--	1 ◇
Dbl	1 ♠	2 ♣	Dbl*
3 ♣	3 ◇	Pass	Pass
4 ♣	Pass	Pass	??

* Support double - an artificial way to show three-card trump support

This one will be fun. We will be able to use the LAW to come up with a very definite conclusion.

Let's do our trump counting. Our support double told our partner that we have three spades. Subsequently, he competed in diamonds. This tells us that he has only four spades because if he had five of them, he would have competed in spades instead of diamonds.

How about his diamond length? Easy to figure out. Let's start by thinking about his *heart* length! If he were 4-4 in the majors, he would have responded one heart, not one spade, to our opening bid. Therefore, he can't have four hearts. He has exactly four spades and at most three hearts. That leaves at least six places in his hand for minor-suit cards.

More reasoning is coming. After all, bridge is a game of logic, and the players that can reason "If *a* then *b*, if not *c* then *d*, etc." are the winners.

We know partner has six or more minor-suit cards. What if he were 3-3 in the minors? That would make him 4-3-3-3. Look at the auction. Would he bid three diamonds with that shape? No! He didn't know we had a five-card diamond suit; from his point of view we could have been 3-4-4-2. He had to have at least four diamonds to make his three-diamond raise.

So, we know partner has exactly four spades and at least four diamonds. He is probably either 4-3-4-2 or 4-2-4-3. Based on his distribution, we have nine diamonds and they have nine or 10 clubs for a total of 18 or 19 trumps/tricks. What about adjustments?

If we were to adjust, everything points towards extra tricks. We have all of our "minor honors" in our side's suits and a very pure hand. This looks like one of those deals where there is quite likely one more trick than the number of trumps. Our Q J x of spades will mesh very nicely with some holding like K 10 x x. We have nothing in their suit -- everything in our suits. Given that there are 18/19 trumps, we should expect 19/20 tricks.

By now, you realize that we have a clear four-diamond bid. We expect that either they're making four clubs, or we're making four diamonds. At the table a reasonable player chose to pass with the South hand below, and he went -130 instead of +130 when this was the full deal:

Dlr: South　　　　　♠ K x x x
Vul: None　　　　　♡ Q x x
　　　　　　　　　　◇ K x x x
　　　　　　　　　　♣ J x

♠ A 10 x x　　　　　　　　　　　♠ x x
♡ K J x x　　　　　　　　　　　♡ 10 x
◇ 10　　　　　　　　　　　　　◇ x x x
♣ A x x x　　　　　　　　　　　♣ K Q 10 9 x x

　　　　　　　　　　♠ Q J x
　　　　　　　　　　♡ A x x x
　　　　　　　　　　◇ A Q J x x
　　　　　　　　　　♣ x

West	North	East	South
--	--	--	1 ◇
Dbl	1 ♠	2 ♣ *	Dbl**
3 ♣	3 ◇	Pass	Pass
4 ♣	Pass	Pass	*Pass*

* Three clubs would have been my choice
** Support double (3 trumps)

East guessed the hearts and scored 10 easy tricks. North-South, with a loser in each side suit, also have 10 tricks available in diamonds. It's no surprise that there are 20 tricks on this 19-trump deal. South should have been able to count the trumps based on the bidding, made a positive adjustment, and thus, the proper four-diamond decision.

At a regional in Dallas, a few of my teammates suffered from ignorance of the LAW. Playing in a knockout match, my partner held:

♠ 10 8 7 5 4 3　♡ K Q 2　◇ 7 6 3　♣ A.

In third seat with both sides vulnerable, he opened one spade. I like the practice of opening light in third seat, so I agree with this one-spade bid. It serves to take away the one level from the opponents. The auction continued:

Larry		Partner	
Pass	Pass	1♠	Dbl
2♠	3♣	??	

More and more players are starting to use conventional two-level raises after a takeout double.[4] In my regular partnership the raise to two spades would show a very weak three-card raise (4-7 points). With this particular partner we were playing no special conventions, so my raise to two spades showed three trumps and 6-10 points.

---

[4] For example, 1♠ (Dbl) 2♣ is used to show a good three-card raise. "B.R.O.M.A.D." (Bergen Raises of a Major after a Double) is described in Better Bidding with Bergen, Volume II.

My partner passed, and the three-club bid was passed around to me. I was looking at:

♠ K Q 2 ♡ 9 8 7 3 ◇ A 5 2 ♣ 10 5 2.

I'm sure, by now, you can predict my action. Never one to violate the "eight-and-eight" rule, I passed, and we were -110 as this was the full layout:

Dlr: North   ♠ K Q 2
Vul: Both   ♡ 9 8 7 3
              ◇ A 5 2
              ♣ 10 5 2

```
        ♠ A J                    ♠ 9 6
        ♡ J 10 4                 ♡ A 6 5
        ◇ K Q 10 9               ◇ J 8 4
        ♣ K J 7 6                ♣ Q 9 8 4 3
              ♠ 10 8 7 5 4 3
              ♡ K Q 2
              ◇ 7 6 3
              ♣ A
```

My partner led a spade against three clubs. Declarer won and knocked out the trump ace. My partner crossed to me in spades, and I played the nine of hearts, declarer ducked, and partner won the queen. Unfortunately, the contract was unbeatable. Partner couldn't profitably continue hearts, and when I later won my ace of diamonds, declarer was then in a position to discard his other heart loser on the fourth diamond. He lost a trick in each suit and made his contract.

How would we do in three spades? We're off a trick in each major suit and two diamonds -- so, we have nine easy tricks for +140. Nine trumps and nine tricks for each side.

I hate to consistently be a pain in the neck, so I didn't bother asking my partner why he failed to bid to the three level with nine trumps. No doubt, he was bothered by the vulnerability. At matchpoints, I might understand his failure to bid three spades, since it is easier for the opponents to double at that form of scoring. If we were making only eight tricks, minus 200 would not be a desirable result. We were playing IMPS, and when your side has nine trumps, the opponents are unlikely to double you in a part-score. We lost 6 IMPS on the deal when, after the same start at the other table, the South player LAW-fully competed to three spades and scored +140.

Later in the match, another deal arose which piqued my interest:

Dlr: South
Vul: None

	♠ 9 4 3	
	♡ 5 2	
	◇ A K Q J	
	♣ K 7 5 3	
♠ A K 8 7		♠ 10 6 5 2
♡ J 8 6		♡ 10 9 3
◇ 7 5 3		◇ 10 9 6 4
♣ Q 8 2		♣ 6 4
	♠ Q J	
	♡ A K Q 7 4	
	◇ 8 2	
	♣ A J 10 9	

South	West	North	East
1♡	1♠	Dbl*	3♠**
4♣	Pass	5♣	ALL PASS

* Negative
** Weak

A short auction, but full of points for me to make!

First, a diatribe about four-card overcalls.

Mike Lawrence, one of the best authors in the game, is a big advocate of the four-card overcall in bridge. It's often the only way to get into auctions at low levels; for example, you hold:

132

♠ A 2 ♡ K Q J 9 ◊ K 8 7 3 ♣ 5 4 2.

Your right-hand opponent opens one diamond, and you have the wrong shape for a takeout double; thus a one-heart overcall is made with only a four-card suit.

Being a big LAW advocate, I try hard to avoid four-card overcalls. Even though I would make an exception with the above hand, I try not to do what West did in the above deal. I want to know how many trumps my partner has. When he overcalls, I expect five cards from him, and then bid to the appropriate LAW level in competitive situations. The problem with a four-card overcall can be seen in the above auction. East's preemptive jump to three spades is not supported by the LAW.

However, East-West were lucky to escape unpunished. South, one of my teammates, did a bit of LAW violating of his own. Instead of venturing to the four level, he should have doubled. As usual, doubles in this kind of situation do *not* show a trump stack. When the opponents have bid and raised a suit, doubles are not for penalty. In this particular auction the double should simply show a hand with extra values. North would then be delighted to pass the double, expecting the LAW to be in his favor.

Why should North convert the double for penalties? North might infer from East-West's bidding that East-West have nine spades; he wouldn't know that South has a doubleton. Even so, he knows that his side has at best an eight-card fit. If South doubles three spades, he doesn't have a five-card minor, so his side won't have more than an eight-card fit. There are at most 17 trumps; nine for East-West and eight for North-South.

With 17 trumps, why should North attempt to buy the contract? If his side can take, say, 11 tricks in five-of-a-minor, then the opponents would have only six tricks in three-spades doubled. On the actual deal, because of the four-card overcall, there are only 16 trumps, and East-West get massacred if they play the hand. The defense has eight top tricks for +800, and only the lucky (unlucky?) lie of the spades prevents them from being able to uppercut another trick.

Instead of collecting that juicy penalty, South ended up misguessing the club queen for -50 in five clubs. It goes on and on! These people are *supposed* to know the LAW. Why are they playing in 4-4 fits on the five level, when they could be defending against a 4-4 fit on the three level? WARNING to all future teammates of mine: please make sure there are lots of trumps present when you venture above the three level in competitive auctions!

Chapter 11 - Newspaper LAW

I'm going to give you a momentary rest from the LAW and present you with two non-LAW related bidding problems. Soon after that, you will learn what's up my sleeve!

First, with nobody vulnerable, you hold:

♠ A J 10 9 6 5　♡ K 8　♢ J 8 7 5 2　♣ --,

and your RHO opens one club. You choose to over-call one spade, and LHO jumps preemptively to three clubs. Your partner bids three hearts, which should be played as forcing. In general, all new-suit bids after the opponents have preempted should be forcing. It's your call:

RHO	You	LHO	Partner
1♣	1♠	3♣	3♡
Pass	??		

You might choose to rebid your spades, or maybe you'd bid four diamonds. Then again, you might raise to four hearts. It's not clear.

Now, the second bidding problem. With neither side vulnerable, you hold:

♠ K ♡ A Q J 6 3 ◇ K 9 3 ♣ 8 7 5 4,

and hear the following auction:

LHO	Partner	RHO	You
1♣	1♠	3♣*	3♡
Pass	4◇	Pass	??

* weak

Would you raise to five diamonds? Would you be happy about the auction? Who knows? It's certainly no fun to bid over preempts.

The astute reader has no doubt realized that these two preceding hands were facing each other, and this was the full deal:

Dlr: East
Vul: None

```
                    ♠ K
                    ♡ A Q J 6 3
                    ◇ K 9 3
                    ♣ 8 7 5 4
        ♠ 7 4                     ♠ Q 8 3 2
        ♡ 10 7 2                  ♡ 9 5 4
        ◇ 10 6 4                  ◇ A Q
        ♣ K J 9 6 3               ♣ A Q 10 2
                    ♠ A J 10 9 6 5
                    ♡ K 8
                    ◇ J 8 7 5 2
                    ♣ --
```

136

This deal appeared in the *Los Angeles Times* syndicated column, written by Alfred Sheinwold and Frank Stewart. I know this is not a book on card play, but to talk about only bidding theory gets boring at times, and the play was interesting. So . . .

South played in four spades with a club lead. Declarer ruffed the club lead and crossed to the king of spades. Next he played a heart to his king, followed by the ace and jack of trumps. East now made the good play of a heart, cutting declarer's communications. Declarer started to run hearts, but East ruffed the fourth round, declarer overruffed and led diamonds. East won and was able to force declarer's last trump out with a club play. As declarer had nothing left in his hand except diamonds, East got in again and had club winners to cash to defeat the contract.

Sheinwold and Stewart pointed out that declarer missed his chance for 10 easy tricks. He can start trumps with the ace, crashing dummy's king, and then drive out the queen. The defense cannot stop declarer from taking five spade tricks and five heart tricks. Cute hand, but what does it have to do with the LAW?

It has to do with the LAW because of the absence of a certain bid. And the absence of that bid annoys me!

I'll tell you why. This was the bidding diagram:

East	South	West	North
1♣	1♠	Pass!!!	2♡
Pass	3♢	Pass	3♡
Pass	3♠	Pass	4♠
ALL PASS			

The exclamation points are mine. Where was West with his obvious three-club preempt? Now, in all fairness to the columnists, they are pitching to an audience, many of whom play West's jump to three clubs as strong or invitational.

But we all know that the jump should be played as preemptive. We also know that the LAW screams for us to make such a bid with the West hand. West knows that his side has at least eight clubs, and his opponents are almost certain to hold an eight-card major-suit fit. His hand is also very pure; all the high cards are in clubs. It's virtually impossible that a three-club contract is not LAW protected. If three clubs goes down, it's almost a sure bet that North-South could have made some two-level contract.

I just get frustrated when I watch North-South have a lovely investigative auction, reaching the best contract. I'd much prefer to see them have to deal with the problems over a three-club preempt that I presented at the start of this chapter. How did you like having to solve those two problems above? The North-South in the diagram were lucky; they got to have a nice, quiet, investigatory auction.

Whenever I read about bridge and see auctions in which a player failed to make a LAWful raise, I get upset, especially when no mention is made of it. I hope that, when you read auction diagrams, you will take note of a player who just sits there passing when, instead, he should be obstructing.

There is sometimes a media bias to ignore such *pass*ivity, but as soon as someone makes an aggressive preempt and goes for 1100, it gets mentioned! If I were to write about the above auction, West would get the full brunt of my wrath. By now you know that I would say, "Over South's one-spade overcall, West decided to jump to 'pass'!"

Chapter 12 - Avoiding Voids

Voids. They have a special place in LAW theory. Simply put, don't defend with voids. That may be a bit too simple, but it's a good partnership guideline.

Try very hard to avoid high-level takeout doubles with voids. Instead, prefer to make a suit-overcall or a notrump-takeout bid.

Also, be exceedingly cautious about leaving in a double with a void.

First, we'll look at a few of these "void-avoidance" auctions, and then I'll explain why you should strive extra hard to not defend with a void. For all problems, assume that nobody is vulnerable.

1) Your right-hand opponent opens four hearts:

♠ K Q 9 7 6	Opponent	You
♡ --	4♡	??
◇ A 9 7 3 2		
♣ K 10 4		

Bid four spades - don't make a takeout double.

2) You open one diamond with the following hand, and partner doubles their four-heart overcall:

You	LHO	Partner	RHO
1♢	4♡	Dbl	Pass
??			

♠ A 8 2
♡ --
♢ K Q J 10 8 7 3
♣ Q 9 2

Remove partner's double to five diamonds - don't pass.

3) Your opponents preempt three clubs and raise to four clubs, and you are holding:

LHO	Partner	RHO	You
3♣	Pass	4♣	??

♠ K 9 5 3
♡ A Q 9 8 3 2
♢ K 6 2
♣ --

Bid four hearts - don't double.

4) You open one spade, and LHO's two-club overcall is passed around to you:

You	LHO	Partner	RHO
1♠	2♣	Pass	Pass
??			

♠ K Q J 9 8 7
♡ Q 9 5
♢ K J 5 2
♣ --

You suspect partner has a trump stack and is hoping you'll double, but, you should bid two spades.

Why are we always pulling doubles with a void? Why are we avoiding takeout doubles with voids? Are we using the LAW? Yes, we definitely are. We are choosing not to defend with voids because the opponents probably have enough trumps to be protected by the LAW.

A double of a high-level preempt is typically played as takeout. Even doubles of four-heart or four-spade opening bids should not be played as penalty. It's just too unlikely that your side will have enough length and strength in trumps to penalize an opponent who has announced a long, strong suit!

When we make these high-level takeout doubles, our partner will be faced with a tough decision. Should he pass and hope to beat the contract, or should he remove the double?

When responding to a takeout double you should "place" partner with 4-4-4-1 distribution. Assume the doubler has a singleton in the preempt suit, and then make the appropriate LAW decision.

If the takeout doubler has a void, or a long suit, this will upset the apple cart. The doubler's partner will too often leave the double in, and the opponents will have enough trumps to be LAW sufficient. For this reason, you should strive hard to avoid doubling with voids!

You should also avoid leaving in doubles with voids. Let's go back and look at each of the above problems. What would be the likely result of defending with a void?

In the first problem, your right-hand opponent opens four hearts, and you hold:

♠ K Q 9 7 6 ♡ -- ◇ A 9 7 3 2 ♣ K 10 4.

If you make a takeout double, what will your poor partner do with:

♠ J 8 5 ♡ Q 7 5 ◇ K 8 4 ♣ Q J 7 2?

If he obeys the LAW he will pass. He expects nine trumps for the opponents, and at most eight for his side. Don't forget -- he's mentally placing you with 4-1-4-4. With at most 17 trumps he'll leave in your double. Opposite your actual hand there are 18 trumps and a positive adjustment for the void. Your five spades and zero hearts are a real surprise. Don't ambush your partner! Bid four spades yourself.

On the second problem, you opened one diamond with:

♠ A 8 2 ♡ -- ◇ K Q J 10 8 7 3 ♣ Q 9 2.

Your partner doubles their four-heart overcall and it's up to you. What does partner's double show? In most partnerships it simply shows "cards." For the majority of hands this is clearly the best approach. What else can responder do with balanced or semibalanced hands with approximately nine or more points? You can't go introducing four or five-card suits at such a high level!

You expect your partner has a few hearts, but it's certainly unlikely he has as many as four. The opponents have at least 10, maybe 11 or more hearts. Your side could easily have 10 or 11 diamonds. Furthermore, as you know, a void is a positive adjustment factor; it suggests more tricks than trumps. Also, in all of these high-level void problems, the opponents have a long suit; that means another positive adjustment. There could easily be 20 or more tricks on this deal, and you have an easy pull to five diamonds. A typical hand for partner would be:

♠ Q J 5 3 ♡ J 8 2 ◇ A 5 2 ♣ K J 5.

Of course, if he has ♡ K Q 10 8 x, you'll have to hear about it for the next 10 years.

On the third problem we are faced with:

Opponent	Partner	Opponent	You
3♣	Pass	4♣	??

♠ K 9 5 3   ♡ A Q 9 8 3 2   ◊ K 6 2   ♣ --.

Again, you should avoid doubling with a void. Partner will assume you are roughly 4-4-4-1, and he will LAWfully leave the double in with a hand such as:

♠ J 10 2   ♡ K 7 4   ◊ Q J 7 3   ♣ Q 10 2.

Instead of scoring +420 or +450, you'll wind up +100 or +300. (Or, on a bad day, -510!) With 19 trumps you'll feel pretty silly not bidding four hearts over four clubs.

On the final problem, you opened one spade with:

♠ K Q J 9 8 7   ♡ Q 9 5   ◊ K J 5 2   ♣ --.

A two-club overcall was passed back around to you. Many experts will disagree with me on this one; they feel that double is the correct call here. As they expect their partner to have a club stack, they want to double so their partner can leave it in.

Experience and the LAW tell me that those experts have it wrong. True, partner "has to" have a trump stack. Since our RHO didn't raise, he can't have too

146

many clubs; this leaves our partner with club length. However, even if partner has five trumps, the opponents will still be LAWfully okay on the two level. Besides, this type of hand is very difficult to defend. Against doubled partscores you usually want to lead trumps through declarer and take away dummy's trumps. On this deal, you are void of trumps. A typical layout is:

```
Dlr: East          ♠ 10 3
Vul: None          ♡ J 10 8 6 2
                   ◇ A 10 9 4
                   ♣ 8 5
        ♠ 6 4                      ♠ K Q J 9 8 7
        ♡ K 7 3                    ♡ Q 9 5
        ◇ Q 8 3                    ◇ K J 5 2
        ♣ A J 7 4 3                ♣ --
                   ♠ A 5 2
                   ♡ A 4
                   ◇ 7 6
                   ♣ K Q 10 9 6 2
```

You	Opponent	Partner	Opponent
1♠	2♣	Pass	Pass
??			

Your partner will be delighted to leave in a double of two clubs. He'll lead the six of spades, and declarer will probably duck the first trick. At this point in the defense you would normally lead a trump through declarer, trying to remove dummy's ruffing value. Unfortunately, you have no trump to play.

Declarer would eventually play his third spade towards dummy. All the defense can do is take two trump tricks, and one in every suit. Declarer will score four trumps tricks, three aces, and a ruff in dummy for +180. East-West are entitled to at least +140 in a spade partial.

If East had a singleton club, it would be much easier to defeat two clubs doubled. With his void, East should do his best to avoid defending.

Chapter 13 - Local LAW

The local NY/NJ double knockouts -- every year -- many of them. There are the North Jersey Double Knockout, the South Jersey Double Knockout, the Westchester (in New York State) Double Knockout, the Long Island Double Knockout, and the Von Zedwitz (in New York City) Double Knockout.

Each match of approximately 28 boards is scored by IMPS. Your team plays against another team every few weeks or so, and stays in the event until it's lost two such matches -- thus, a double knockout.

These events seem endless. Fortunately, I've had the good sense never to be the team Captain. He or she is the one who must endure the continual headaches of trying to find a mutually convenient date and place for 8-12 people to play a bridge match. Good thing for answering machines and call waiting.

In the 1993 North Jersey Double knockout, we were facing a competent team in the finals. Several deals into the match, with nobody vulnerable, in second seat, I held the following:

♠ K ♡ J 9 7 5 ◇ K 8 4 3 ♣ Q J 7 3.

I heard a one-notrump opening on my right, showing 12-15. As much as I love to disturb the opponents' notrump, this hand would be pushing it. Even if I were silly enough to bid, which suit (or two suits) would I show?

I reluctantly, but sensibly, passed, and after responder's natural two-heart bid, my partner overcalled with two spades. What should I do? To my way of thinking, partner was in the "balancing seat." My LHO's two hearts was a sign-off, so partner didn't need much for his two-spade bid. This was described in the section on OBAR BIDS[5] in *To Bid or Not to Bid*. Should I pass or try two notrump?

No doubt, you are wondering what this has to do with the LAW, and you are right to wonder. I didn't face this decision. My RHO raised to three hearts, a somewhat unusual action in that two hearts was a "drop-dead" bid.

It's not clear what a double by me would mean in this situation. Normally such doubles, when the opponents bid and raise a suit, are played as card-

---

[5] **O**pponents **B**id **A**nd **R**aise, **B**alance **I**n **D**irect **S**eat.

showing[6] -- not as penalty. But, I didn't want to punish my partner for "balancing," so I passed it around to him, and he doubled!

RHO	Larry	LHO	Partner
1NT (12-15)	Pass	2♡	2♠
3♡	Pass	Pass	Dbl
Pass	??		

Clearly, his double was for takeout. Not only did I know this from my heart length, but generally when a player overcalls and then doubles, he is showing a hand with something like 6-1-3-3, with the singleton in the opponents' suit. A more recognizable example might be:

West	North	East	South
1♡	1♠	2♡	Pass
Pass	Double		

On the deal in question, I had to decide whether to pull the double or leave it in. Most players, when presented with this problem, chose to make a four-heart cuebid. They loved our "fit" and the fact that

---

[6] Throughout this book a card-showing double is used to indicate a hand that has values, but no suit to show. The player is stuck for a bid, but needs to do something; so a double shows "cards." Some people refer to these as "action doubles."

all of our points were outside of hearts, where partner had shortness. They were willing to play in four spades or five of a minor; whatever partner decided would be fine. Other players pulled to three no-trump, trusting that jack-fourth of hearts would stop the suit, although I'm not sure why.

You, of course, are not guessing what to bid. You're thinking about the LAW. You assume partner is not void in hearts. In the previous chapter, I cautioned against such things. Let's see what the situation would be if partner is 6-1-3-3.

We would have seven trumps, and they would have eight for a total of 15 tricks. Yikes! Bidding would be crazy.

What if partner had some other shapes? We will now have an eight-card fit in a minor, for a total of 16 trumps. Maybe he has 5-5 and we will even have a nine-card fit, for a total of 17. Still, we expect to beat three hearts doubled. Why should we bid? If we have enough tricks for a game, we will slaughter three hearts.

I was very amused that many experts answered this problem with a call other than pass. I love it when the LAW leads to a clear-cut, winning decision, while a good player's instincts would have led him astray.

I passed, partner led a trump, and dummy tabled a very good hand:

Dlr: North
Vul: None

♠ Q 9 7 2
♡ A K Q
◇ 9 6 5 2
♣ A 10

♠ A J 8 5 3
♡ 8
◇ A J
♣ K 9 6 5 2

♠ K
♡ J 9 7 5
◇ K 8 4 3
♣ Q J 7 3

♠ 10 6 4
♡ 10 6 4 3 2
◇ Q 10 7
♣ 8 4

The play was complex, but we ended up defeating three hearts doubled four tricks for +800. It's true that a four-heart cuebid by me would have led to a five-club contract and +400, but defending three-hearts doubled was much better. There were 17 trumps, more than we expected, but pass still was the big winner. Perhaps North shouldn't have gone to the three level with his spade length and only eight trumps.

In the same double knockout match, I had another LAW decision; this one involving Precision. If you're not familiar with Precision, don't let that bother you; the LAW is still applicable.

Vulnerable against not, I opened a strong and artificial club, holding:

♠ A 9 8 5 2 ♡ A J ◇ A K 9 8 4 ♣ 3.

A nice hand with 16 high-card points, clearly worth a Precision one-club opening. I always get a little bothered when people hear the alert to one club and are told it is Precision. They then ask, "How many high-card points does it promise?" I wouldn't get annoyed at a new player for asking, but an experienced player should realize that "high-card points" are not the key. Wouldn't you open a strong, forcing, and artificial *two* clubs with:

♠ A Q ♡ A K Q J 9 8 7 x ◇ K x ♣ x?

It's "only" 19 high-card points! However, you probably would open only one heart with this 20-point hand:

♠ K J x ♡ K J x x x x ◇ K Q ♣ A K.

At any rate, I deemed the above 16-count a big club, and my partner responded with a negative (artificial) one diamond. For those of you who count points, it shows 0-8.

I was now surprised to hear a one-spade overcall!

One of my suits. I chose to pass, as double would be for takeout in our methods, and it went two spades on my left! Now my partner, bless him, doubled for takeout. I was about to pass gleefully, but I decided that I better first check with the LAW:

Larry	LHO	Partner	RHO
1♣ (Prec.)	Pass	1◇ (0-8)	1♠
Pass	2♠!	Dbl (takeout)	Pass
??			

First of all, as you now know, you should usually try not to play your partner for a void when he makes a takeout double. With a void he should try hard to make some other sort of takeout bid. In this case, however, as you're looking at five spades, there is a chance he has doubled with a void.

Let's suppose the opponents have 7½ trumps, since we're not sure whether they have seven or eight. Let's also guess that our partner has four diamonds. Three or five are both possible, but four is statistically most likely. That yields 7½ + 9 = 16½ trumps/tricks.

What about adjustments? Hard to say. If partner has a spade void, our ace could be wasted. On the other hand, our cards argue for purity if partner has a hand such as:

155

♠ x ♡ K Q x x ◇ Q x x x ♣ x x x x.

Everything will be a useful working card.

I decided to see what the LAW suggested if there were 17 trumps/tricks. Remember that we were vulnerable against not at team scoring.

If we defeated two spades, by three tricks, that would mean that they took only five tricks. Five plus *twelve* equals 17, so we would have a diamond slam! If we beat them only two tricks (+300), they would have six tricks, translating into *eleven* for us. Hence, we would have a diamond game (+600).

With only 16 trumps, it wouldn't be so clear to bid; you can go through the numbers.

So, in this example, the LAW didn't give a clear-cut answer. However, I decided that 17 trumps was a good estimate as there were probably positive adjustments. I had no minor-honors in spades, and all my cards would fit partner well. I cuebid three spades, and we eventually ended up in six diamonds. This was the full deal:

Dlr: North   ♠ A 9 8 5 2
Vul: N-S   ♡ A J
                 ◊ A K 9 8 4
                 ♣ 3

♠ K Q J 10 7   ♠ 6 4 3
♡ 8 4 2   ♡ Q 7 6 3
◊ 5 3   ◊ J 10
♣ A J 6   ♣ K 8 7 4

                 ♠ --
                 ♡ K 10 9 5
                 ◊ Q 7 6 2
                 ♣ Q 10 9 5 2

My partner played the hand well (that always helps!) and emerged with 12 tricks and +1370.

Can I credit the LAW with this super result? Not necessarily; I had to guess to use 17 as the number of tricks. However, the deal is published here to illustrate one further type of auction in which the LAW can come into play.

Chapter 14 - Doubled Partscores

Leaving in doubles of partscores is not my idea of fun. I suppose it's fun if I have a trump stack, but what I'm talking about are the situations where the LAW seems to indicate you should defend, but your stomach doesn't quite feel up to it. For example, you hold:

♠ x x x   ♡ 10 x x x   ◇ Q J x   ♣ x x x.

With nobody vulnerable, your RHO opens three hearts, which is passed around to your partner. "Double," he says, and you have a decision to make.

You have no place to go -- no suit that you really want to bid -- and three notrump doesn't look too appetizing. By the way, I don't like three notrump because I have no tricks. It's not because I'm worried about them running hearts -- the opening bidder doesn't rate to have AKQJxxx. (As long as partner has a heart -- even a small singleton -- the suit will probably be blocked for the defense.)

If partner is 4-1-4-4, our usual starting point for LAW usage, there are eight hearts and seven of our suit for 15 trumps. Perhaps there are 16 tricks, due to the positive adjustment for the long suit. This number usually argues for defending. The problem is that we're terrified that the opponents have nine of those 16 tricks. We have very little defense. Who wants to go minus 530?

Is there an answer to this dilemma? Not really. I suspect that in the long run, the winning action is to pass. You will indeed go -530 a fair amount of the time. However, there are many occasions on which you'll get +100 or +300 for passing, as opposed to a minus score for bidding.

If my hand were slightly changed to:

$$\spadesuit \, x\,x\,x\,x \quad \heartsuit \, 10\,x\,x\,x \quad \diamond \, Q\,J\,x \quad \clubsuit \, x\,x,$$

I would be delighted to pull the double to three spades. Now I can expect 8+8 or 16 trumps, plus one for the same positive adjustment, and a total of 17 tricks. One side could have nine and the other eight, which makes it okay to bid. When I have a *clear* place to run I give up making the risky leave-in for penalties.

How would you judge this one?

$$\spadesuit \, J\,9\,6 \quad \heartsuit \, 6\,5\,2 \quad \diamond \, Q\,8\,7 \quad \clubsuit \, A\,J\,6\,5,$$

with both sides vulnerable:

RHO	**You**	**LHO**	**Partner**
2◇ (weak)	Pass	3◇	Dbl
Pass	??		

I faced this decision in the 1994 Cavendish Pairs.[7]

As I've already stated, I don't like to leave in take-out doubles of partscores. In the last example, with a four-card major, I had a clear place to escape; this time I was in a quandary. Should I bid three-of-a-major with only three cards in the suit? How about four clubs? Three notrump, anyone?

This kind of problem is often seen in bidding panel features in magazines. These days, with more and more total-trick awareness, the majority vote is usually for pass. On a panel of 30, you might get 12 votes for pass, and 6 each for three-of-a-major, three notrump, and four clubs. What's right?

There is no "right." We just want to do what will give us the best expectancy in the long run. I'd guess that a pass would lead to -670 one time in five. Bidding on probably leads to a minus score 60-70% of

---

[7] This annual event has a Calcutta style auction that raises more than one-quarter of a million dollars. Part of the pool is donated to charity, and the rest goes to the players and bettors. The scoring is done by IMPS across the field of 20 or so tables.

the time. You could run a simulation (if you have a computer and the proper bridge software), or you could do an expected value calculation.[8]

Do I go through all these calculations at the table? No, bridge is a timed event! What I do calculate is how many trumps/tricks there rate to be. This takes no time at all. I always "project" partner to have 4x1. In this case, they'll have nine diamonds and we'll have eight clubs, for a total of 17. My queen of diamonds could easily be a trick on defense, but not offense. After adjusting, I'd expect 16½ tricks. This clearly argues for passing. The most likely scenario is that neither side can make anything at this level. Sure, on my bad days they might have nine tricks, and I'll sheepishly have to write -670 on my score card. But, I just had to do what I thought was the long-run winning action, based on the LAW, so I passed and led a heart. This was the full deal:

---

[8] Say that you think passing will lead to -670 one time in five. Three times in five you will be +200, and the other time in five you will be +500. Then your expectancy for passing is:

-670	x	20%	=	-134
+200	x	60%	=	+120
+500	x	20%	=	+100

Expectancy for passing = + 86 points

For bidding, you'd do the same calculations. Say that 3-of-a-major would make +140 60% of the time, and -100 30% of the time, and -200 10% of the time, etc.

Dlr: East
Vul: Both

```
                    ♠ K 10 8 4
                    ♡ A K 10 8 7
                    ◇ 4
                    ♣ K 10 3
    ♠ A Q 7 2                    ♠ 5 3
    ♡ J 4                        ♡ Q 9 3
    ◇ J 5 3                      ◇ A K 10 9 6 2
    ♣ Q 9 4 2                    ♣ 8 7
                    ♠ J 9 6
                    ♡ 6 5 2
                    ◇ Q 8 7
                    ♣ A J 6 5
```

Declarer lost two club tricks, two hearts, and one in spades and diamonds for down two, and +500 to the good guys. This turned out to be a very congenial layout from my point of view! Can our side make anything? Three notrump is down after the expected diamond lead. Four clubs is very ugly, and it probably wouldn't make. Three spades is touch and go. (No one ever said it would always be easy to determine how many tricks each side has on best play and defense!) The only plus score that could come from pulling the double would be if South guessed to bid three hearts, and North judged not to raise to four. I'd expect nine tricks in hearts. Notice that they had seven tricks in diamonds, for a total of 16 tricks if both sides play in their best fit. There were 17 trumps, but look at all of the "minor honors!"

So, I survived the leave-in, but I have to admit that I didn't enjoy myself until after I saw the dummy and the first few tricks. Applying the LAW in this kind of situation can give you gray hairs and ulcers.

The theme for this kind of decision is:

Usually, there are three or four possible places to pull the double. However, only one of them is likely to lead to a makeable contract. If you were always able to find that correct spot, then pulling the double would be the winning action. However, the odds aren't in your favor; you'll probably guess to pull to the wrong spot. So, it's generally better to take your chances on defense.

Of course, you'll want to have a sympathetic partner and understanding teammates when you do occasionally go minus 670.

Would you risk an ulcer on this next one?

♠ Q 9 7 6   ♡ 8 4   ◇ K 10 7   ♣ K 10 7 2

You are playing IMPS, vulnerable against not, and your LHO opens three clubs. Your partner doubles, RHO passes, and it is up to you.

Let me divert your attention for a moment and give you some background information on this problem.

I enjoy reading the "auction problem solving" sections in the various bridge magazines. For years, the *Bridge World's* Master Solvers Club has been my favorite. In this column, eight problems are posed to a panel of experts. Their answers are printed, along with comments explaining their bids. The reader gets to see how the panel voted and to study their opinions.

Now that the LAW of Total Tricks is gaining adherents, you can often find references to it in the panelists' comments. The above bidding problem comes from the June 1993 IPBM Macallan Bidders' Club.

♠ Q 9 7 6 ♡ 8 4 ◇ K 10 7 ♣ K 10 7 2

West	North	East	South
3♣	Dbl	Pass	??

Unfortunately, you can't know how many trumps there are, but, as I always do in this type of situation, I mentally assign partner a 4-4-4-1.

Here, we would come up with the typical eight-and-eight three-level situation. We are guessing eight clubs for them and eight spades for us, and as we know from the LAW, that indicates defending. Their possession of a long suit (clubs) is a positive adjustment, but that is offset by our "minor honors" in clubs, a negative adjustment.

I was surprised, but very pleased to see, that the top vote getter was pass. I don't think you would have found as many passers before the LAW started to gain in popularity. The final vote was:

Pass	-	13 votes
3NT	-	12 votes
3♠	-	5 votes

Some typical comments made by the panelists were:

Joey Silver: *Pass. The 'LAW' says if we can make nine or 10 tricks in notrump or spades, these boys are in big trouble right here at the three level, so why spoil a good thing by opening up my big mouth.*

Max Rebattu: *Pass. . . . I have no excellent alternative . . .*

Sally Horton: *It is true that 300/500 may be inadequate against the right game, but is there any guarantee that any other action will reach the right game?*

These last two comments point out the very common problem which was outlined in the box above. If you are fortunate to guess the right contract after your partner doubles a preempt, you might score better than if you choose to defend. However, you usually must choose from among one of several possible bids; but, with only one of them will you do better playing than defending. It's usually better to take +100 or +300 than to occasionally guess +140 or +620, but often go -100.

I still honestly hate to be faced with hair-raising leave-ins of doubles. However, if the LAW says to leave it in, then I close my eyes and hope for the best. What do you think of this one?

♠ J 8 6   ♡ 10 9 7 5   ◇ 10 8 7 2   ♣ 9 8 ?

Vulnerable against not you hear:

Partner	**RHO**	**You**	**LHO**
1 ♠	2 ◇	Pass	Pass
Dbl	Pass	??	

Am I serious? Not really. This one is easy. Although you have four of their suit, you have an easy two-spade bid. (Two hearts is possible, but I prefer the known eight-card fit.) The problem continues . . .

Partner	RHO	You	LHO
1♠	2♦	Pass	Pass
Dbl	Pass	2♠	Pass
Pass	3♦	Pass	Pass
Dbl	Pass	??	

Partner has a good hand, and is again inviting your decision.

This deal comes from Barry Rigal's excellent book, *Test Your Bridge Judgment.* He suggests a three-heart bid, which buys the contract. He then spends several pages describing the very intricate play of the hand:

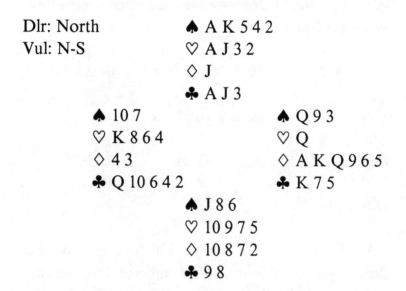

Dlr: North
Vul: N-S

```
                    ♠ A K 5 4 2
                    ♡ A J 3 2
                    ◇ J
                    ♣ A J 3
      ♠ 10 7                      ♠ Q 9 3
      ♡ K 8 6 4                   ♡ Q
      ◇ 4 3                       ◇ A K Q 9 6 5
      ♣ Q 10 6 4 2                ♣ K 7 5
                    ♠ J 8 6
                    ♡ 10 9 7 5
                    ◇ 10 8 7 2
                    ♣ 9 8
```

Eventually, declarer comes home with nine tricks for +140. Back to the bidding.

While I understand the pull of the second double, I just have to get my two cents in about the LAW. North's shape is just what South might expect, and that means 8 + 8 = 16 trumps. The ten of diamonds will become a minor honor (trick on defense not offense) any time that North's singleton diamond is the jack, queen, or king. Working the other way is the probable double fit.

On the actual deal, three diamonds doubled has no chance. It is off two top spades and one of everything else. The defense also has excellent chances for an additional trick to set the contract two tricks. Meantime, three hearts was quite a struggle.

Am I suggesting that South should leave in the double of three diamonds? It's certainly possible, as there is a good chance that each side has eight trumps. On a bad day North might have doubled with a diamond void (he should try not to!), and I don't want to defend opposite that. On other days, we simply won't have enough strength to take five tricks against three diamonds doubled. There could be 16 total tricks, but they might be split nine for them, and seven for us! I do suspect that pass is the correct action, but it's just too hard (and nerve-wracking) to play the game that way. I'd probably make the same cowardly pull of the double as did Mr. Rigal's South player. Call me a hypocrite if you must.

170

Chapter 15 - Florida LAW

January is a good time to be in Florida. Take a seat in the Orlando regional. You're playing matchpoints against strong opponents. Vulnerable against not, you deal and open one club with the following collection:

$\spadesuit$ Q 6 $\heartsuit$ K 9 8 4 $\diamondsuit$ Q 5 $\clubsuit$ K Q J 8 2.

Your partner makes a negative double of LHO's one-heart overcall, and RHO raises to two hearts. You pass, and LHO raises to three hearts.

You	LHO	Partner	RHO
1$\clubsuit$	1$\heartsuit$	Dbl (neg.)	2$\heartsuit$
Pass	3$\heartsuit$		

In today's world of preemptive or "barrage" bidding, this raise is not invitational; it is simply used to take up room so the opponents cannot explore. It is analogous to what people call "1-2-3 bar."[9] There are many other ways for LHO to invite his partner to four hearts. Almost all hands with six hearts warrant

---

[9] In the auction: 1 Major - 2 Major - 3 Major by a partnership - the last bid is a "bar" bid, not invitational to game. It's used to make it difficult for the opponents to get into the auction.

this "bar-bid." Even some five-carders, such as:

♠ K x x x ♡ A Q 10 x x ◇ x ♣ x x x,

would be possible. The three-heart bidder suspects that his opponents have a nine-card minor suit fit, and he wants to make it difficult for them. He knows that the LAW will protect him. If his opponents can take nine tricks with their nine trumps, he will be down only one in three hearts. He hopes his opponents will misjudge and go to the four level, or that they'll have trouble finding their best fit.

Your partner doubles three hearts. This is not a penalty double; it simply shows a desire to compete, a hand with extra values, something like:

♠ A J 9 x ♡ x ◇ A J x x x ♣ 10 x x.

Having already made a negative double, partner is stuck for a bid over their three hearts. He has no suit to bid, but has too many high cards to pass. Given the fact that the opponents have bid and raised a suit, all doubles in this type of situation are used to show extra values, not a trump stack. Competitive bidding should not allow for pure penalty doubles based on a trump stack when the opponents have a known fit. The card-showing double is much more essential.

Armed with all of the above bidding theory, it is time for you to make your decision:

♠ Q 6 ♡ K 9 8 4 ◇ Q 5 ♣ K Q J 8 2

South	West	North	East
1♣	1♡	Dbl (neg.)	2♡
Pass	3♡	Dbl (cards)	Pass
??			

The analysis above should have been enough to point you in the right direction. The opponents are almost a lock to hold exactly eight trumps; their bidding assures that they have more than seven. Partner would be very unlikely to double with a void -- after all, he'd probably have some suit to bid and couldn't risk your leaving in the double if he knew the opponents had nine trumps. Thus, partner has one heart, they have eight. From his negative double, partner has four spades; otherwise, he would have bid one spade over one heart. His distribution is most likely 4-1-4-4 or 4-1-5-3. With five clubs he would probably have raised clubs instead of doubling three hearts, although doubling would be LAWful if opener were 3-4-3-3, yielding only 16 trumps. So, we know that they have eight hearts, and we have eight or nine clubs, for a total of 16 or 17 trumps and tricks. If we can make four clubs (10 tricks), then three hearts doubled will yield only six or seven tricks. We have a clear pass of partner's double.

The full deal:

Dlr: South   ♠ A K J 5
Vul: N-S   ♡ 7
                ♢ K 10 8 4 2
                ♣ 6 5 3

♠ 10 8 4 2   ♠ 9 7 3
♡ A Q 10 5 2   ♡ J 6 3
♢ 6   ♢ A J 9 7 3
♣ A 9 4   ♣ 10 7

                ♠ Q 6
                ♡ K 9 8 4
                ♢ Q 5
                ♣ K Q J 8 2

Against three hearts doubled, your expert partner would lead a trump. The best declarer would be able to do is to ruff a club loser in dummy. He'd lose one heart and five black-suit tricks for a total of only seven tricks. If declarer times the play very well, he might escape for down one by scoring five hearts in his hand, two aces, and a ruff in dummy. North-South can take only nine tricks in clubs. They're off three aces and a diamond ruff. That diamond ruff which defeats four clubs is the same trick that prevents

East-West from going down even more in three hearts doubled.

Was West's three-heart bid silly? No, definitely not. Against many opponents he would not only get away with it, but he'd also end up with a good score for pushing his opponents into a minus score on the four level. Against others, he would survive if he didn't get doubled. On the actual layout, against expert LAW users, he'd be sorry he ever saw this deal!

Down the Florida Turnpike in West Palm Beach, playing with my great aunt in a club game, I pick up:

♠ Q 9 x x   ♡ K x x   ◇ A 9 8 x x   ♣ A.

Nobody is vulnerable and I deal and open one diamond. My partner, who is quite inexperienced, responds one notrump. My RHO overcalls two hearts, and it's up to me:

Me	LHO	Partner	RHO
1 ◇	Pass	1NT	2 ♡
??			

My matchpoint instincts are telling me not to pass. I just hate to go quietly on these low-level partscore

175

auctions. All indications are that the points are fairly evenly divided. I have 13 and my partner has 6-10; so our side has 19-23 points, and they have 17-21 points. This deal is very unlikely to be played in game by any pair at any table.

The traveling score slip will be filled with scores such as 50, 90, 100, 110, 120, 130, 140, etc. If I pass two hearts and it becomes the final contract, I won't expect a very good score. Minus 110 certainly won't be good since we likely could go -50 or -100 if we play the hand. Even +50 won't be a great score if we can make something our way.

As much as I hate passing, I don't have a very obvious bid to make. Two spades is tempting, but I really should have a bit more in the way of high cards or spade cards. Two spades is kind of a "reverse," but it shouldn't promise a great hand. Although I think two spades is the tactically correct matchpoint action, I don't think I could convince too many people to bid it.

What other calls are available besides two spades? How about three diamonds? No, too unilateral -- I'd be guessing that my partner had some diamond support. What if partner is 3-3-2-5 in that order? We'd be in a seven-card fit at the three level! Maybe if my hand were:

♠ x x x ♡ x x ◇ A Q J 10 9 ♣ A Q x,

I could perpetrate a three-diamond bid with only a five-card suit. I'd know (from partner's one-notrump response) that the opponents have at least eight hearts. However, with my actual ace-empty-fifth and possession of three hearts, I can't really contemplate it.

We haven't yet considered a double. What would a double mean? In "standard," double would be for penalties -- we certainly don't have enough for that. In today's world, some pairs play a double in this situation as takeout, while others play it as "cards" -- asking partner to do something. However, without discussion, double would be played as penalty.

Thus, I reluctantly passed. It's nice if you can make your pass in tempo so that your partner does not have any ethical problems later in the bidding. You don't want her to know that you had a problem. Fortunately, I did manage to make my pass without huddling, and LHO passed likewise. My partner, bless her, reopened with three diamonds.

Have you noticed that I haven't mentioned the LAW yet? Must be some kind of record, all this analysis of a partscore auction without even one mention of my beloved principle. How is this deal governed by the LAW?

Our partner, for her one-notrump response, has at most three hearts. If she had three hearts and a decent hand, she should double two hearts. The exact meaning of such a double (a one notrump response to a minor, followed by a double of a two-of-a-major overcall) is: maximum values, and usually three cards in their suit.

Her actual three-diamond bid doesn't deny three hearts. She might bid three diamonds with four-card support, regardless of her heart length. So, our partner's heart length is a bit of a mystery -- she can have one (very unlikely given a one-notrump response), two, or three! We don't know if the opponents have seven, eight, or conceivably even nine trumps. Our partner rates to have three or four diamonds, so we have eight or nine trumps. Now you know why I didn't mention the LAW. It's not very useful on this deal; it's too hard to gauge the number of trumps. In general, we try to approximate, but here we have quite a wide range, since there could be anywhere from 15 to 18 trumps/tricks!

Just as an aside, this is another example of how the "LAW bashers" denounce the LAW. They say that "the LAW is silly -- no one knows how many trumps anyone has." Yes, it's true that, on this deal, the LAW is not very valuable in the bidding. But, so what?? We won't use it this time.

My partner's three-diamond bid is passed around to LHO who doubles. I don't mind this -- I have a very good hand for partner, a fifth diamond, and a well-placed king of hearts. But, alas, RHO pulls to three hearts. I'm tempted to double, but leave well enough alone, and three hearts becomes the final contract. I lead the ace of clubs, and see this dummy:

Dlr: West
Vul: None

♠ x x x
♡ J 10
♢ K J 10 x x
♣ K J x

♠ Q 9 x x
♡ K x x
♢ A 9 8 x x
♣ A

West	**North**	**East**	**South**
Me	LHO	Partner	RHO
1 ♢	Pass	1NT	2♡
Pass	Pass	3 ♢	Pass
Pass	Dbl	Pass	3♡
ALL PASS			

Yikes! -- that's some diamond suit in dummy!

My partner encourages in clubs, but alas, I can't continue that suit. I consider a spade shift but ultimately realize that it will serve no good purpose. I exit passively with a trump, and partner surprisingly produces the ace! She shifts to the eight of spades; declarer wins the ace and plays another trump. I win the king, partner following, and exit safely with a trump. Declarer runs a few trumps and then plays king of spades, jack of spades. I win my queen as partner shows out, and I get off lead harmlessly with another spade. As declarer has three small clubs, he still has another club trick to lose for down one, the full deal being:

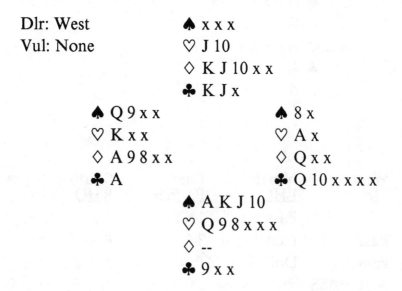

Dlr: West
Vul: None

♠ x x x
♡ J 10
◇ K J 10 x x
♣ K J x

♠ Q 9 x x
♡ K x x
◇ A 9 8 x x
♣ A

♠ 8 x
♡ A x
◇ Q x x
♣ Q 10 x x x x

♠ A K J 10
♡ Q 9 8 x x x
◇ --
♣ 9 x x

Notice that a spade switch at trick two would have allowed declarer to make the hand. He'd play on trumps and eventually throw me in with the fourth spade. I'd have to play a diamond, giving him his king of diamonds for his ninth trick.

After the deal, my LHO asked me, "What does the LAW say about this hand?" I am frequently asked questions like this when I play at a local bridge club. Usually, I have a good answer, but this was one of those "difficult-to-analyze" deals. I love it when you can look at the diagram and say: "North-South have x tricks, East-West have y tricks, etc." On some deals, such as the one above, it's just too complicated. How do North-South do in diamonds? Ugh! What is the best way to time the hand? Who has the seven, six, and five of diamonds? Conveniently, I no longer remember. On to the next hand!

One hour south down I-95 and I'm playing in a Swiss Team event in Miami. It's the first match of the day, and we're opposing a team I expect to beat. They are very old-fashioned and sound bidders, yet I'm confronted with a preempt. In fourth seat, at unfavorable vulnerability, I am sitting South holding:

♠ K 5 3 ♡ A K 4 2 ◇ 10 ♣ K Q J 8 4.

Two passes are followed by two hearts, presenting me with a difficult decision. I could pass, bid three clubs, or overcall two notrump. There are arguments for all three actions, but I prefer two notrump; the only major problem being the singleton. However, as the auction continues, my real problem is yet to come:

West	North	East	South
Pass	Pass	2♡	2NT
3♡	Dbl*	Pass	??

* Negative

My LHO has raised to three hearts, and my partner has made a "negative" double. This shows some values (at least six or seven points) and usually four cards in the other major.

Being a LAW aficionado, I'm tempted to pass without thinking any further. I've learned through LAW usage that passing a double when holding four of the enemy's trumps is almost always winning action. Could this be an exception? I ask my LHO what the chances are that his partner has opened on a five-card suit. He laughs and says that he's been playing with his partner for 10 years and he's never had fewer than six! My favorite kind of opponent.

Usually when I ask my opponents about their methods, I get responses such as "I don't know -- we never discussed it," "I never saw the guy before," or even, "No hablo inglés." This time, I had gotten one of those rare honest answers; I knew that my RHO had six trumps. LHO probably had three for his raise, so they had nine. Of course, there was a possibility that LHO had only two trumps or that RHO had gotten into the spirit of things, making his first five-card preempt of the decade. This would give the opponents only eight trumps.

Let's look at some of our partner's possible shapes:

4-0-5-4	4-0-4-5
3-0-5-5	4-1-4-4
3-1-5-4	3-1-4-5
4-1-3-5	4-1-5-3

As we can see, he's very likely to hold at least four clubs. There rate to be nine hearts for them and at least nine clubs for us -- 18 total trumps and tricks. It could be 17 or 19, but 18 feels like a good guideline to use.

We must also consider notrump and the LAW. One of our possible calls is three notrump. Just to review, the notrump formula says to add seven to the opponents' number of trumps, $9 + 7 = 16$ total tricks. If we can make nine tricks in three notrump, +600, then they will have seven tricks, and we will get +300 for passing. This seems to indicate that three notrump is a better call than pass.

What if we bid four clubs? With 18 total trumps, if three hearts doubled were to go down only one (+100), then we would have 10 tricks in four clubs (+130). If three hearts were going down two (+300), then partner probably has a decent hand and would raise us to five clubs. We would have 11 tricks (+600), since they have seven tricks.

Whether we should opt for three notrump or a move towards a club game is not clear. But we can certainly conclude that pass is not the correct call:

```
Dlr: West        ♠ J 7 6
Vul: N-S         ♡ --
                 ◇ A K J 8 3
                 ♣ 10 7 6 5 2
    ♠ A 10 8 2              ♠ Q 9 4
    ♡ 10 7 6               ♡ Q J 9 8 5 3
    ◇ Q 9 7 4             ◇ 6 5 2
    ♣ A 9                  ♣ 3
                 ♠ K 5 3
                 ♡ A K 4 2
                 ◇ 10
                 ♣ K Q J 8 4
```

As you can see, if we had passed the double, the result would have been down two for +300. The defense would take three diamond tricks, two hearts, and eventually a spade.

Five clubs is an easy make; declarer has to lose only to the two black aces. There are 11 tricks in clubs plus seven tricks in hearts, for a total of only 18 tricks, in spite of the 19 trumps. This is due to the duplication of the ace-king of hearts opposite a void. Although AKxx was not listed in chapter four as "minor honors," it represents a negative adjustment on this deal. The ace and king are sure tricks on defense but, on offense, opposite shortness (especially a void) they will often be wasted.

Three notrump is also an easy make since the diamond finesse works -- nine tricks in notrump (four clubs, three diamonds and two hearts) for us and seven in hearts for the opponents, for a total of 16. The notrump formula predicted this result accurately; nine, their number of hearts, plus seven, the number we always add.

When I faced the decision at the table, my instincts were telling me to pass. Fortunately, after asking LHO about the preempt, I decided on 18 Trumps. Following the LAW, I knew that I should not leave in the double, and I chose to pull to four clubs, which partner raised to five. I took 11 easy tricks for +600.

Chapter 16 - Italian LAW

I love to play bridge abroad. The world bridge community seems to be more enthusiastic about "bridge at the top" than here in America. Many countries invite top American partnerships to play in their tournaments. Not just invite, but pay all the expenses, and then treat them like royalty during their stay!

In September of 1993, my partner David Berkowitz and I were invited by the Italian Bridge Federation to play in one of the most scenic settings of our bridge careers. The sight was a town called Campiogne, nestled in the Alps on the Swiss-Italian border.

Perhaps I spent too much time looking out the window at the lakes and mountains because we did not do very well in the tournament. I could also blame the following deal, where I held:

♠ 10 9 2 ♡ K Q 9 6 4 ◇ 7 3 ♣ K 8 2.

In an IMP Pairs game, with both sides vulnerable, I was presented with this problem:

David	RHO	Larry	LHO
1♠	Pass	2♠	Pass
Pass	2NT (minors)	Pass	3♣
Pass	Pass	??	

There aren't *any* countries left in the world where they let you play in two spades! No matter where you are, you should never let your opponents play on the two level with an eight-card fit. Our opponents balanced themselves into three clubs, and I decided that the LAW said to Pass. I assumed eight trumps for each side, and I try not to bid "three-over-three" in such situations. I passed, and this was the full deal:

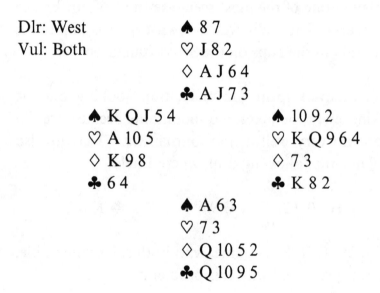

Dlr: West
Vul: Both

```
                ♠ 8 7
                ♡ J 8 2
                ◇ A J 6 4
                ♣ A J 7 3
  ♠ K Q J 5 4              ♠ 10 9 2
  ♡ A 10 5                 ♡ K Q 9 6 4
  ◇ K 9 8                  ◇ 7 3
  ♣ 6 4                    ♣ K 8 2
                ♠ A 6 3
                ♡ 7 3
                ◇ Q 10 5 2
                ♣ Q 10 9 5
```

The declarer in three clubs scored an easy +110, losing only the four obvious tricks. Very nice decision by North to bid two notrump -- although I might have chosen to balance by doubling with his hand.

As it turns out, we can also make three spades. Each side had eight trumps as I suspected, but both sides had *nine* tricks! Why is this so? For one thing, there is a double fit. For another, the deal turns out to be pure. Every card pulls its full weight on offense and defense. Notice that if I had the ten of diamonds (instead of declarer), we would at least have defeated their contract. We would have taken two heart tricks and one in every other suit.

Perhaps I could have gotten this one right. It appeared from the bidding that there was a reasonable chance for a double fit on this deal. As North announced both minors, the actual shape of David's hand should not have come as a surprise to me. The deal seemed very pure -- I had no queens or jacks or tens in their suits. I probably should have added one trick for these positive factors, for a total of 17 trumps/tricks. Then I would have been able to make the winning three-spade (or three-heart) call.

The tournament was won by Dario Attanasio and Giuseppe Failla from Sicily. Late in the event Dario was faced with an interesting bidding decision. With

IMP scoring, vulnerable against not, he held the following hand:

♠ A J 8 6 ♡ Q 9 ◇ A 4 ♣ K Q 8 4 3.

His RHO dealt and opened with a Precision two-club bid. In this case it promised 11-15 high-card points and five or more clubs. Attanasio might have chosen to overcall with a natural two notrump, but elected to pass. The responder also passed, and Failla balanced with a takeout double.

RHO	Attanasio	LHO	Failla
2♣	Pass	Pass	Dbl
Pass	??		

Attanasio thought a long time. He had to consider whether to pass, settle for a spade game, or try for a spade slam. Three notrump was also vaguely possible.

Thinking about slam wouldn't really be fair to his partner. Attanasio really didn't want to bury Failla for balancing. Sure, he could cuebid once or twice, but it's very unlikely he'd be getting to six. Even if he did, he'd presumably be off the ace of clubs. His partner would need to cover every other loser in his hand. There also could be trouble in handling all of the clubs.

That's already too much reasoning. It's time to consult the LAW. I know that the anti-LAW crowd gets annoyed at such statements. "How can you consult the LAW when you don't know how many trumps anyone has?" they protest. "We hardly ever *know* for sure; we are using the LAW as a guideline," I reply. As you know, in this kind of takeout double auction, I like to assign partner 4-4-4-1 with a singleton in their suit. No, we can't expect that to be his exact shape, but it will give us a good starting point.

In this case, if partner is 4-4-4-1, we would figure on eight spades for us and seven clubs for them for a total of 15 trumps and tricks. Keep in mind that partner could have zero or two clubs and might have three or five spades, so the number of trumps doesn't have to be 15. But, I would guess it is 14, 15, or 16 at least 90% of the time. That is why assuming 4x1 gives us a very good ballpark estimate.

Let's see what the number 15 tells us. If we reach four spades and make 10 tricks for +620, we will expect to hold them to five tricks in two clubs doubled for +500. I could make a negative adjustment; if I did, I would subtract from the trick count due to my club holding. My club suit will probably produce tricks on defense, but not necessarily as many on offense. Adjusting suggests that if there are 15 trumps, there will be fewer than 15 tricks.

For the time being, we'll continue with our estimate of 15. Let's see what happens if we get to four spades and take more or less than 10 tricks. Try going through the math yourself. Did you find any way to split the 15 tricks to make the score for bidding four spades better than the score for defending two clubs doubled? The only situation is if there are exactly 10 tricks for us and five for them. Even in that case the gain is minimal, +620 instead of +500.

What if there were 14 or 16 trumps? There is no need to go through the math. As you become more familiar with the LAW, you'll realize that <u>if you have decided that you should pass with a certain number of trumps, then</u> **you should always pass if there are** *fewer* **trumps.** In other words, if the LAW tells you to PASS with 15, then with 14 you should definitely PASS as well. Conversely, <u>if you have determined that is right to bid with a certain number of trumps, then</u> **you should always bid if there are more trumps**. If 17 trumps suggest that you BID, then, by all means, you should be BIDDING if there are 18.

So, on this example, with 15, 14, or 13 trumps we should PASS.

With 16 trumps, bidding four spades will be right if we have 10 or 11 tricks (+620 vs. +300, or +650 vs.

+500). If we have 9 or 12 tricks then passing would be right (+100 vs. -100, or +800 vs. +680).

So, what does the LAW say we should do? With 16 trumps, we could go either way. With 15 or 14 trumps we should definitely defend. So, 2½ out of 3 cases suggest defending. The LAWful solution to this problem is indisputable; we should pass.

Notice that we never did assess precisely the total number of trumps. How could we? Because the percentages told us that pass was the winning call for most distributions, we didn't need to know the exact number. Pass had to be the winning call.

You might want to see what the LAW says about bidding three notrump. Remember that the no-trump/LAW formula says to add seven to the number of trumps; in this case we are assuming they would be playing in a seven-card club fit. Thus, the total-trick number would be 14. If we were to make nine tricks in three notrump, +600, we could expect them to take five tricks in two-clubs doubled, +500. That is the only case where bidding three notrump would be better than defending.

The full deal isn't relevant, but I'm sure that after enduring all of that logic you would like to see it. And I'll show it to you in a moment.

Whether or not pass was the winner in real life is irrelevant. I suspect that pass would work out about 75% of the time. I could "rig" the deal so that pass works; after all, how many people reading this will have played at the Campiogne tournament?

This is a book on bidding. I don't believe that any competitive decisions come with a guarantee. Just because the LAW concludes that an action is correct, it doesn't mean that it will work on the actual deal. I've tried to give a proper blend of deals showing, in general, how effective the LAW is. Of course, there are times where it fails us. However, in my experience the LAW is overwhelmingly the way to go. I dare anyone to prove otherwise!

All right, enough preaching. Here is the actual deal from Campiogne:

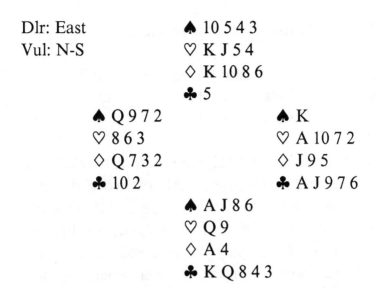

Dlr: East
Vul: N-S

```
                    ♠ 10 5 4 3
                    ♡ K J 5 4
                    ◊ K 10 8 6
                    ♣ 5
   ♠ Q 9 7 2                    ♠ K
   ♡ 8 6 3                      ♡ A 10 7 2
   ◊ Q 7 3 2                    ◊ J 9 5
   ♣ 10 2                       ♣ A J 9 7 6
                    ♠ A J 8 6
                    ♡ Q 9
                    ◊ A 4
                    ♣ K Q 8 4 3
```

On most deals the LAW works but on some it doesn't. This deal fits into what I would call a third classification; the "difficult-to-analyze" category.

Don't forget that the LAW of Total Tricks assumes best play and defense. Yet, that's not always so easy to determine!

I can tell you that this deal was played in four spades at six tables and that only one North-South pair managed to make it. To analyze the play in four spades is beyond the scope of this book, but suffice to say that the four-one break was too difficult to handle. West usually scored two trump tricks to defeat the contract.

Now, back to our original auction.

East	Attanasio	West	Failla
2♣	Pass	Pass	Dbl
Pass	*Pass*	Pass	

Failla made a very bold, but probably the choice of most experts, balancing double of two clubs, and Attanasio eventually decided to pass. I don't know if he used the LAW or his judgment, but his side ended up +500 (the play was involved and tedious). This result went a long way towards helping them win the event.

Chapter 17 - DONTing Away

Readers of *To Bid or Not to Bid* send me an endless quantity of mail. The most frequent letters ask questions about "DONT," a conventional method of Disturbing Opponents' NoTrump.

DONT is a catchy acronym for a Marty Bergen convention which everyone should play! It has been responsible for an exorbitant number of good results over the years.

Briefly, the purpose of DONT can be summed up with just the "D." DISTURB! It is unbelievably right to get in the way when your opponents open a strong notrump.

Just as an aside, many players have also asked about DONT against weak notrumps. I still recommend DONT, although you should only interfere with decent hands (opening-bid strength or better).

Since our goal is to disturb, we want to be able to do so as safely as possible. IMPORTANT WARNING! We are not trying to get to game! We are merely trying to find a safe haven, preferably with total-tricks protection.

After a one-notrump opening double is used to show any one-suited hand. Forget about penalty doubles; they are useless! All they do is help the opponents scramble into a better spot if they are in trouble. Defending one-notrump doubled usually results in -180 after you (like I always do) guess to make the wrong opening lead.

Your DONT double asks partner to bid two clubs, and you pass with clubs or pull to your suit. Pulling to spades shows a very good hand. Otherwise, a direct two-spade overcall is used for weak spade one-suiters.

Aside from two spades, the other two-level over-calls show two suits. Which two you ask? Well, that's very easy to remember. One of the suits is the suit you bid. Two clubs shows clubs and any other suit. Two diamonds shows diamonds and any higher suit (a major). Two hearts shows hearts and a higher suit (obviously spades).

D.O.N.T. AFTER OPPONENTS' 1NT

Double = One suit

2♣ = ♣ + ANY OTHER SUIT (4-4 or better, usually at least 9 cards)

2◊ = ◊ + EITHER MAJOR (4-4 or better, usually at least 9 cards)

2♡ = ♡ + ♠ (4-4 or better, usually at least 9 cards)

2♠ = ♠ (weaker than double followed by 2♠)

The responder to the DONT overcall should use common sense. He passes if he is content, or tries to scramble to another suit. With three-card support, generally the responder should pass; otherwise, he should run to a better spot. It would take many pages to cover all the possible nuances of scampering into (hopefully) a fit, but suffice to say that good logic and a safety-first approach[10] will handle 95% of the situations. The other 5% will undoubtedly result in a letter to the author!

A more detailed schedule of responses to DONT can be found in Appendix C.

What do you need to make a DONT overcall or double? Not much more than the 13 cards you were dealt. In fact, just make sure your partner is in on the joke so that he will act prudently. At unfavorable vulnerability try to be a little more cautious.

One of my friends loves to get carried away with DONT. In spite of my warnings, he uses DONT at every legal opportunity. He once overcalled two clubs in direct seat, (vulnerable against not, no less!) with:

♠ A J x x ♡ x x x ◇ x x ♣ K J x x.

I don't remember the exact deal, but I promise you that we got a good result! No, I don't advocate such recklessness. However, he's yet to pay for one of these brash bids. It's unbelievable how often his

---

[10] Don't make heroic attempts to find the perfect contract. You might have to settle for a 4-3 fit, even though a 4-4 fit might be available. Also, instead of playing in a major-suit contract, you might have to play in a lower-scoring minor-suit one. The goal is to play any undoubled contract. You are often way ahead of the game by virtue of having been able to enter the bidding safely.

interference turns -90 or -120 into a better score. I'm sure that one of these days he'll turn it into -800, but as we already have so many good ones in the bank, it won't hurt so much.

I believe it is imprudent to bid with that hand in direct seat at unfavorably vulnerability. However, in balancing seat I would do so routinely; yes, even at those awful colors. No, I don't expect the cognoscenti to agree, but perhaps they'll start making mental notes of the success of such actions. It's amazing how right it is to balance against one notrump on almost every hand. Well, . . . maybe it shouldn't be so amazing.

As you know, the "notrump/LAW" formula states that total tricks equals seven plus the number of trumps. So, if we can scramble into an eight-card fit (DONT gives us a better chance than any other method), there will be 15 tricks. Quite often they can make one notrump, and we can also make two of our suit. Even if we land in a seven-card fit, more often than not we will end up with a better result, something like -50 instead of -90, +90 instead of +50, or +110 instead of +100 is commonplace.

One of the best reasons for balancing is to prevent those awful opening leads our partners usually make. They always lead our short suit against one notrump.

Do they hate us? No, it just makes sense from a probability point of view. Your partner will lead his longest suit. Since he has four or more, the notrump opener has at least two, and dummy tends to be relatively balanced, how many does that leave for you? Too often, partner will lead from Q 10 x x x into your small doubleton, costing your side a trick:

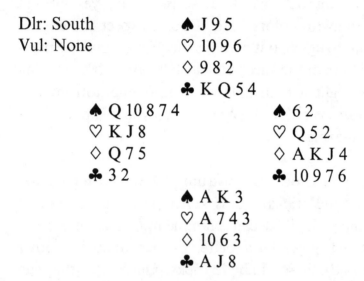

Dlr: South
Vul: None

```
                    ♠ J 9 5
                    ♡ 10 9 6
                    ◊ 9 8 2
                    ♣ K Q 5 4
  ♠ Q 10 8 7 4                   ♠ 6 2
  ♡ K J 8                        ♡ Q 5 2
  ◊ Q 7 5                        ◊ A K J 4
  ♣ 3 2                          ♣ 10 9 7 6
                    ♠ A K 3
                    ♡ A 7 4 3
                    ◊ 10 6 3
                    ♣ A J 8
```

South opens one notrump, and against most players he'd get to play there. West leads a spade, of course, blowing a trick. Declarer scores an effortless +120. If you were East, would you be happy with this result? Wouldn't you rather balance with two clubs, to show clubs and another suit? Sure, you have only 10 points and 4-4 distribution. On the actual deal, you wouldn't even land in a 4-4 fit. Partner would pull to two diamonds, saying, "What's your other suit?" You would pass, and partner would presumably score +90, losing the obvious five tricks. This is a very typical layout, and you'll record an infinite number of good results by playing DONT and balancing aggressively.

One additional advantage of disturbing the opponents' notrump is that many players don't know how to cope with the interference. They have no agreements as to what their bids mean. One exceptional illustration of this occurred after a two-no-trump opening! Yes, I advocate playing DONT even at this high and dangerous level. After a two-no-trump opening, the same reckless friend/student made a DONT three-club overcall with:

♠ 10 9 x x   ♡ x x   ◇ x x   ♣ K J 10 x x!

He was at favorable vulnerability, but I think this is going too far. In any event, the woman on his left was looking at:

♠ K x   ♡ K x   ◇ K Q J 9 x x x   ♣ x x.

She desperately wanted to know how many aces her partner had. Without interference, she would have simply bid Gerber, four clubs to ask for aces. She would then place the contract in five, six, or seven notrump accordingly. Now, she had no idea what to do. She bid four clubs, hoping it was Gerber, but alas, her partner took it as Stayman. How would you play it? Who discusses such things? They ended up in the wrong contract, and yet another victory was scored for DONT.

Enjoy your disturbing, but please go easy if you're ever playing against me and I open one notrump. I like to have a free run!

Chapter 18 - Statistical LAW

Of the many letters I've received from LAW followers, perhaps the most intriguing one was from Edward Schwan, an accounting professor at Susquehanna University in Pennsylvania.

My initial reaction was to cringe when I saw a summation sign (Σ) and lots of charts and formulas.

However, there were a few points that we non-actuaries can understand.

First, he expanded on a subject that was covered in *To Bid or Not to Bid*. He pointed out that if "our" side has nine trumps, there have to be at least 17 total tricks. Sound too simple? We've actually touched on this earlier, but let's again go through the uncomplicated math.

We have nine trumps, and for argument's sake we'll say that our suit is spades. This means that only four of the opponents' 26 cards are spades. Therefore, 22 of their cards are distributed amongst the other three suits. They can't be 7-7-7 . . . that adds up to only 21. Therefore, they must have at least one eight-card fit. We have 9, they have at least 8, so there are at least 17 trumps and tricks.

His second piece of interesting information was a computer simulation for 1,000 deals. He sent this chart which illustrates how many total trumps there were on each deal:

North-South's Number of Trumps

		7	8	9	10	11	12	Tot
E	**7**	105	54	*	*	*	*	159
a	**8**	57	252	103	19	4	*	435
s	**9**	*	119	130	44	7	2	302
t	**10**	*	26	35	21	5	0	87
-	**11**	*	2	11	3	0	0	16
W	**12**	*	*	1	0	0	0	1
est's Number of Trumps	**Tot**	162	453	280	87	16	2	

Across the top of the chart is listed North-South's total number of trumps. Down the left side is East-West's number. At the intersection is the number of deals (out of 1,000) on which the two sides had that number of trumps. For example, at the intersection of 9 and 9, is the number 130. So, on 130 out of 1,000, or 13% of all deals, you would expect each side to have nine trumps.

Notice that the most likely occurrence is eight trumps for each side, which occurs on 252/1000, or slightly more than 1/4 of all deals. It's that "eight-and-eight" situation where you'll find that many people violate the LAW by bidding "three-over-three."

Incidentally, the *'s represent impossible situations. As we've already seen, if one side has nine trumps, the other side can't have 7.

I liked his chart, but would have been really impressed if he told me how many tricks there were on each of those 1,000 deals! Actually, in the 1960's, Jean-Rene Vernes (the inventor of the LAW) attempted such a simulation in his book *Bridge Moderne de La Defense*. Vernes researched several hundred World Championship hands, and found that the LAW was "off" by an average of four-tenths of a trick per deal. I've tried to find out from him if he used adjustments in his analysis. Unfortunately, something got lost in the French translation of "adjustments," and I haven't received a satisfactory answer as of this writing.

Mr. Schwan was most enthusiastic about the last point that he makes. It contains that dreaded summation sign, but he swears that his formula is very simple and most useful.

Alright, here's his formula:

$$\sum \text{Bids} = \sum \text{Total Trumps} - 11$$

His formula is a shortcut to tell you what level to bid to in competition, after you've determined how many total trumps there are.

Let's say that the bidding tells you there are 17 trumps. Your side has a heart fit, and the the opponents have competed up to three clubs. The formula says that "the sum of the bids" should equal 17-11, or 6. This means that you should bid three hearts. The "sum of the bids" should be 6. They've bid 3, and since 3+3 is 6, you are safe bidding on the three level.

Say that the opponents have stopped in two spades. You expect 16 total trumps and want to know if you should compete onto the three level. The formula says 16 - 11 = 5. So, the "total of the bids" should be five. Since they've bid two, your side should compete to three. It's as simple as that.

This formula's biggest flaw is that it does not take vulnerability into account. So, I still suggest using "chart logic."[11]

Using the formula does provide an easy shortcut. Let's look at Mr. Schwan's example:

---

[11] Draw a mental chart as on page 21. Say to yourself: "I expect 16 trumps. If they make 9 tricks, for 140, then our side has 7 tricks, for minus 100, etc."

♠ 7 4 ♡ K 9 5 ◇ Q 10 7 6 ♣ K 9 5 3.

He doesn't give vulnerability, but says that LHO opens one spade, our partner overcalls two hearts, and RHO raises to two spades. He says that the opponents have eight trumps (5+3) and we have eight trumps (5+3) for at least 16. Subtract 11. The "sum of the bids" is five which means we should bid on the three level. He says to bid three hearts with confidence. Naturally, you could come to the same LAWful conclusion without his formula. I would solve his problem by saying to myself: "Since the opponents have eight spades, I don't want to let them play on the two-level."

You should develop your own preferences for LAW usage. While I prefer "chart logic," you might prefer Schwan's formula, or the more simple rules of "eight trumps -- two level," "nine trumps -- three level." However complex you want to make it, please be sure to consult the LAW in all of your competitive bidding endeavors.

Chapter 19 - Seattle LAW

At the 1993 Seattle Nationals, I decided that everything was right with the bridge world. No, not a single victory for me in 10 days, but the LAW seemed to be as alive and well as it had ever been.

The viewgraph commentators didn't let a deal go by without commenting on the total number of tricks. My opponents all kept telling me how much they enjoyed the LAW (not necessarily good for my matchpoint score). And, I couldn't even turn the dummy without thinking about the LAW . . .

In the Reisinger final, my partner, David Berkowitz, opened one Precision diamond and I was looking at:

♠ Q ♡ Q J 8 2 ◇ 10 7 5 ♣ K 9 5 4 2.

With nobody vulnerable, my RHO overcalled one spade, and I made a negative double. The auction continued:

David	RHO	Larry	LHO
1◇	1♠	Dbl	3◇
Dbl	3♠	Pass	Pass
4◇	ALL PASS		

The three-diamond bid was a "mixed raise," showing four trumps and about 7-10 points. It seems everyone is making "total-tricks" bids these days. David's double simply asked for a diamond lead, but his four diamonds made me happy. After all, the opponents had to be content at the three level with their nine trumps.

Now, here is how I "played the dummy."

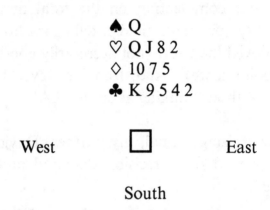

♠ Q
♥ Q J 8 2
♦ 10 7 5
♣ K 9 5 4 2

West   □   East

South

West led a small trump -- small, small, nine. David led a heart -- king, small, small. I already started trying to figure out who can make what. What were David's hearts? Probably two small because no other holding would explain his trick-two play. David was probably 3-2-6-2.

West now took several minutes before emerging with a low spade to the queen, king, and a small one from David. East returned a trump, won by David in hand. He then played another heart to my queen and the ace. The jack-of-trumps return by East was won in David's hand, and it now felt to me that the full deal was:

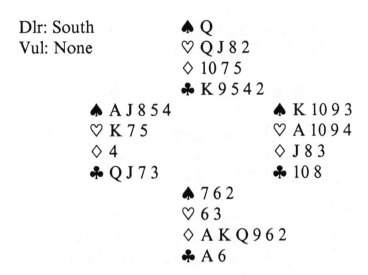

Dlr: South
Vul: None

```
                    ♠ Q
                    ♡ Q J 8 2
                    ◇ 10 7 5
                    ♣ K 9 5 4 2
♠ A J 8 5 4                      ♠ K 10 9 3
♡ K 7 5                          ♡ A 10 9 4
◇ 4                              ◇ J 8 3
♣ Q J 7 3                        ♣ 10 8
                    ♠ 7 6 2
                    ♡ 6 3
                    ◇ A K Q 9 6 2
                    ♣ A 6
```

Without a trump lead, four diamonds would have made easily; however, the opponents had defended well. As David didn't get to ruff any spades in dummy, he ended up with only nine tricks. David could have played spades first, but that would have also led to failure as his heart pitch (for a spade) would not have been set up in time.

Nine trumps and only nine tricks. But I enjoyed my dummy turning because by the end of the deal, I knew that the opponents had nine tricks available in their nine-card spade fit. If their diamonds were two-two, they wouldn't make three spades. But alas, if their diamonds were two-two, they couldn't stop us from taking 10 tricks in diamonds. Try it out! Appreciating the beauty of the LAW -- what a good way to spend your dummy time.

Take the South seat, and see if you can appreciate the LAW on these bidding problems from Seattle:

1) Dealer: West Vul: N-S Matchpoints.

South			
♠ 9 6			
♡ J 7 6 3			
◊ A 9 4 3			
♣ A Q 7			

West	North	East	South
2◊ *	Dbl **	Rdbl***	Pass
2♠	Pass	3♠	??

* Weak two-bid in either major
** Showing opening-bid strength,
   somewhat balanced shape
*** What's your major?

2) Dealer: South Vul: N-S IMPS.

South			
♠ J x x			
♡ A J x x			
◊ x x			
♣ Q x x x			

West	North	East	South
--	--	--	Pass
Pass	1♣	Pass	1♡
Dbl	2♡ *	Dbl **	Pass
2♠	Pass	Pass	??

* Promises four
** Responsive

214

3) Dealer: West Vul: None   Matchpoints.

South	West	North	East	South
♠ K 10 4	Pass	Pass	1♡	Pass
♡ 8	2♣ *	Pass	2♡ **	??
◇ A J 10 7				
♣ J 10 9 6 3	* Drury			
	** Sign-off			

4) Dealer: South Vul: E-W Matchpoints

South	West	North	East	South
♠ 10 8 6 5	--	--	--	1◇ *
♡ 7	Pass	1NT	Pass	2♣
◇ A Q 5 3	Pass	Pass	2♡	??
♣ A 9 8 4				

* We *like* to have more when we open, but this is the way we open anyway! Aggressive is the winner!

Players were confronted with these decisions in National Championship events. These are the kind of decisions that arise in the trenches day after day, and they determine the winners and losers of events.

On problem 1, a National champion in the South seat bid four hearts, and was dismayed to find:

Dlr: West   ♠ A J 8
Vul: N-S   ♡ A K 10
                ◇ K 6 5 2
                ♣ 9 5 4

♠ 10 7 5 4 3 2   ♠ K Q
♡ Q 9 5 4   ♡ 8 2
◇ J 8   ◇ Q 10 7
♣ 2   ♣ K J 10 8 6 3

           ♠ 9 6
           ♡ J 7 6 3
           ◇ A 9 4 3
           ♣ A Q 7

That East-West pair did a bit of LAW-violating themselves by bidding to the three-level with only eight trumps. However, it was South who was the most criminal, as he failed to double three spades. All such doubles in this preempt-crazy world should show "cards," not "pure penalty." North-South ended up down two in four hearts (double-dummy he might have made it), instead of going plus a large number. Bidding "four-over-three" with 15 trumps is not a growth industry.

On problem 2, the South player thought the theme was to compete to the three level based on a potential double fit. However, this was faulty reasoning. In this auction the responsive doubler surely denied four spades. If he had four spades, he would simply have bid two spades in order to play in his known eight-card fit. So, the opponents could be credited with only seven spades on the actual auction. Why were they not bidding diamonds? Presumably, their auction was telling you that they didn't have nine diamonds (or they would have reached three diamonds).

Thus, you know that your partner has at least three cards in diamonds and at least three spades as well (since the opponents don't have eight). Partner also has four hearts. As he opened one club, you can be pretty sure that he is 3-4-3-3. Whew! ... a lot of words, but it should all make sense. This kind of logic is valuable because it will surely help you make LAWful decisions. Knowing partner is 3-4-3-3, you should pass. If you bid three hearts with your eight-card fit, what are you hoping for? If you somehow make it (nine tricks), the opponents will be down two (six tricks) in two spades. More likely, you will both go down. Partner's hand was actually:

♠ K x x ♡ Q x x x ◊ K J x ♣ A x x,

and three hearts was down three, -300!

On problem 3, I hope you recognized the necessity to "pre-balance." The opponents are apparently stopping in two hearts, presumably with eight trumps. Your side is is almost guaranteed to have its own eight-card fit somewhere. Giving partner four hearts, can you arrange his other three suits in such a way as to deny your side an eight-card fit? The only way is if he is specifically 4-4-3-2, and in that case, getting to two spades over two hearts with 15 trumps is no problem. So make a takeout double of two hearts, the LAWful action.

On problem 4, you also want to push them to three hearts. Actually, you hope to buy it for three clubs, but under no circumstances should you allow them to play in two hearts. Don't worry about your high-card minimum -- partner isn't going to punish you. If you pass, you'll be sorry to see them play in two hearts, even if partner has only:

♠ K x x ♡ K x x ◇ x x x ♣ Q x x x.

Can you make three clubs opposite that garbage? No, but you probably won't get doubled, and down two for -100 will still be better than -110 against two hearts. More likely, you'll push them to three hearts and have a shot at collecting +100. You know from partner's one-notrump response that they have a *minimum* of nine hearts, and you have eight clubs for a total of 17 trumps/tricks. Why should you sell out on the two level?

The LAW makes competitive bidding easy. With enough trumps, bid to the appropriate level. Without enough trumps, pass or double. That is the LAW in a nutshell. Following the LAW will make you a winner on all four decisions above and on most decisions you'll ever face at the table.

218

Chapter 20 - Chile LAW

In the 1993 World Championships in Santiago, Chile, I was fortunate to have one of the world's very best players as my teammate. Eric Rodwell already had three World titles under his belt, and I was hoping he'd get his fourth. His quote on the back cover of *To Bid or Not to Bid* reads: "Practical information you'll use the next time you play, and every time you play." He is a friend, a good teammate, and he <u>knows</u> the LAW of Total Tricks. But Eric, dear Eric, why did you do this?

With no one vulnerable, you held:

♠ K 7 5 ♡ 8 6 4 2 ◇ A K 8 5 ♣ K Q.

Your partner opened one notrump (10-13); your RHO overcalled two diamonds, showing a one suiter in a major. You doubled and your LHO, from South Africa, bid two hearts, asking his partner to pass with hearts or correct with spades. Your partner doubled, which was followed by a jump to three spades on your right. You then bid four hearts and played there.

Dlr: North
Vul: None

```
              ♠ Q 10
              ♡ K J 9 5
              ◇ Q J 9 4 2
              ♣ A 7
  ♠ 2                        ♠ A J 9 8 6 4 3
  ♡ 10 7                     ♡ A Q 3
  ◇ 10 6 3                   ◇ 7
  ♣ 10 9 8 6 5 3 2           ♣ J 4
              ♠ K 7 5
              ♡ 8 6 4 2
              ◇ A K 8 5
              ♣ K Q
```

North	East	South	West
Bergen	**S. Africa**	**Rodwell**	**S. Africa**
1NT (10-13)	2◇ (♡ or ♠)	Dbl	2♡ (pass/correct)
Dbl	3♠	4♡	ALL PASS

Against four hearts, West led his singleton spade and received a ruff. East later got his two trump tricks and you were down one. If East had been greedy, he could have beaten the contract two tricks by playing a diamond at trick two. Then, after winning the first round of trumps, he could give West a spade ruff and receive a diamond ruff for the second undertrick.

What was wrong with Eric's bidding? The reason, he says, that he bid four hearts, was "The guy jumped to three spades -- I thought he'd have a good hand, so why double?" Unfortunately, that is the kind of reasoning that world class players often use, when instead they should do a bit of total-tricks thinking. All Eric had to do was add eight to eight. He knew East-West had at most eight spades (his partner promised at least two for his one-notrump opening). He also knew his side rated to have only eight hearts.

Eric should have expected 16 trumps and the same number of total tricks. His poor hearts and king of spades should have argued for even fewer tricks. His king of spades was, indeed, a trick on defense, but worthless on offense. On the other hand, he could also make a positive adjustment in light of the fact that his RHO had a long spade suit. These two factors (one negative and one positive) cancel out, still leaving an expectation of approximately 16 tricks. With that estimate, how could it have been right to bid four hearts instead of doubling three spades?

Eric would have defeated three spades doubled by

two tricks[12] for +300 instead of the -50 he received. I'm pleased to say that he later realized that his four-heart bid was an error, and he also admitted that if he had thought about the LAW, he would have gotten it right.

This story, though, had a happy ending. At the other table the auction took a different turn:

North S. Africa	East Cohen	South S. Africa	West Berkowitz
1NT (12-14)	Dbl *	Rdbl	2♣(Nat.)
Pass	2♠**	Dbl	3♣
Pass	Pass	3NT	Pass
Pass	4♣	Pass	Pass
4◇	Pass	5◇	Pass
Pass	Dbl	ALL PASS	

* One suit
** Stronger than direct two-spade overcall

Of course, I had an easy lead of ace and a spade, followed by two heart tricks and a heart ruff for down three, +500 and a 10 IMP gain! I wasn't sure whether or not to sacrifice over three notrump with

---

[12] If declarer gets to ruff a heart in dummy, he will lose two trumps tricks. If the defense plays trumps, declarer will lose only one trump trick, but will have two heart losers. In either case, declarer is down two.

222

that four-club bid. My instincts told me to bid four clubs, but just to make sure, I used the LAW as a guide. I decided my partner's bidding probably showed a seven-card club suit. We had nine trumps, and using the notrump/LAW formula, I decided that there should be 16 tricks. Furthermore, I made a positive adjustment for partner's seven-card suit, to get close to 17 tricks. If they were making three no-trump (nine tricks), then our four-club sacrifice would not be down more than two (eight tricks). Thus, I knew that bidding four clubs was "in the ball-park." On the actual deal, three notrump was un-beatable (can you see any way to set it?), and four clubs would be down two with the best defense of two rounds of trumps followed by three diamond winners.

Later in the tournament, there was a deal I will never forget. Our American team had to go through months and months of qualifying matches for the ultimate event in bridge, the Bermuda Bowl. In this World Championship contest, we had survived all the way to the semifinals and were in a very close match against The Netherlands. With several deals to go, I held this hand:

♠ 8 5 3 ♡ K 10 9 7 5 ♢ 6 3 ♣ Q 7 5,

with both sides vulnerable. We opposed the youthful Dutch stars, Berry Westra and Enri Leufkens. Berry opened one spade on my right, and after my pass, Enri "raised" to three notrump. This was alerted as showing 7-10 points and 4+ trumps, a distributional raise to four spades. My partner, David Berkowitz, doubled, and Berry duly bid four spades:

Westra	Me	Leufkens	David
1♠	Pass	3NT*	Dbl
4♠	??		

* 7-10 points, 4+ spades

There I was. A LAW of Total Tricks decision was quite likely to determine the winner of the match. My "LAW" instincts told me to pass, while most players' instincts would tell them to bid in this situation. In fact, the deals were duplicated in the other Bermuda Bowl semifinal match, as well as the Venice Cup for women. I later found out that the players faced with a similar decision (often after 1♠ - pass - 4♠ - double) all bid five hearts. I don't know why *they* bid five hearts, but *my* reasoning was as follows:

1) Partner probably has one spade and four hearts. No guarantees, but that is where I will start my thinking.

2) If that is true, then there are nine spades and nine hearts for a total of 18 trumps.

3) So, if they are making four spades, 10 tricks for +620, then our save in five hearts doubled is going down three, eight tricks for -800.

There might have been one more or one fewer trump, but it still didn't seem that there were enough trumps/tricks to warrant bidding five-over-four. Accordingly, I passed, and this was the full deal:

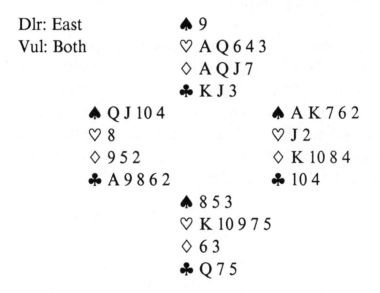

```
Dlr: East        ♠ 9
Vul: Both        ♡ A Q 6 4 3
                 ◊ A Q J 7
                 ♣ K J 3
   ♠ Q J 10 4                 ♠ A K 7 6 2
   ♡ 8                        ♡ J 2
   ◊ 9 5 2                    ◊ K 10 8 4
   ♣ A 9 8 6 2                ♣ 10 4
                 ♠ 8 5 3
                 ♡ K 10 9 7 5
                 ◊ 6 3
                 ♣ Q 7 5
```

David had *five* hearts, so there were actually 19 trumps. Were there 19 tricks? We have 10 tricks -- losing one in each side suit, down one if I had bid five hearts. East-West have to lose one club, one heart, and two diamonds, assuming we lead them before the clubs are established. That's a total of nine tricks for them, down one in four spades. We had 10 tricks and they had nine for a total of 19, equalling the 19 trumps. So, bidding five hearts would turn a plus into a minus.

The LAW worked perfectly -- five hearts was down one in the other room, four spades was down one at our table. We won 5 IMPS and went on to win the match by 13, surviving to meet Norway for the World Championship.

Hold everything. This is revisionist history. The LAW did not work perfectly. In real life things were ever so slightly different. I really did pass four spades, and my Dutch counterpart at the other table did indeed bid five hearts. But alas, the jack and eight of diamonds were interchanged. The full deal in Santiago was actually:

Dlr: East   ♠ 9
Vul: Both   ♡ A Q 6 4 3
                ♢ A Q 8 7
                ♣ K J 3

♠ Q J 10 4   ♠ A K 7 6 2
♡ 8   ♡ J 2
♢ 9 5 2   ♢ K J 10 4
♣ A 9 8 6 2   ♣ 10 4

                ♠ 8 5 3
                ♡ K 10 9 7 5
                ♢ 6 3
                ♣ Q 7 5

How did this little swap of the eight/jack affect the
LAW? Five hearts was still down one, off the same
three tricks. However, four spades was cold. Declarer had only *one* diamond loser, and thus, we were
-620. Our teammates were +100 against five hearts,
undoubled. Alas, instead of winning 5 IMPS on the
deal, we actually lost 11 and ended up losing the
match by 3 IMPS! And, The Netherlands went on to
beat Norway in the finals and won the 1993 World
Championships.

What's the point? The LAW is not perfect. Slight
variations such as the eight/jack of diamonds in the
above deal can cause the total-trick count to be off in
one direction or the other. The LAW caused me to
pass four spades, but maybe I should have used it a

bit differently. Instead of thinking: "Partner has one spade and four hearts for a total of 18 trumps, therefore, pass," maybe I should have thought: "Partner might have five hearts which means 19 trumps. With 19 trumps it would be wrong to bid only if the tricks were split exactly 10 for us and nine for them, as in my first imaginary layout."

Furthermore, my hand argues for a purity adjustment of +1 -- no "minor honors," etc. Thus, there could be 20 tricks, in which case it has to be right to bid since one side will definitely be making its contract and a game bonus. On the actual deal, there were in fact 19 trumps and 20 tricks due to the total purity of the deal. Every card pulled its full weight on offense.

Also, I shouldn't have presumed that five hearts would be doubled. Even if it was down two or three against a cold four spades, it would show a huge profit at minus only 200 or 300 versus minus 620.

Again, I ask "What's the point?" The LAW is a guideline. There is very often a gray area where you are not sure exactly how many trumps there are or what adjustments to make. On any deal, there could be one trick more or less than expected due to the random vagaries of the placement of an eight or a jack. On the above deal I probably should have followed the adage "when in doubt, bid one more."

Does this mean that the LAW is useless? No, the LAW is as useful as it has ever been. I'm simply illustrating what can go wrong. Many people read *To Bid or Not to Bid* and expected that the LAW was etched in stone. The LAW is a wonderful tool that everyone should use. But, like anything in bridge, the LAW isn't perfect; it won't always work. No matter how much you love the LAW, it will sometimes fail you.

Have you ever gotten a bad result when you used Stayman? Or Blackwood? Of course, but I'm sure you still use both Stayman and Blackwood. Don't give up on the LAW. It's always there to protect you and to keep you from making irrational bidding decisions.

Thank you for joining me on my journeys to the local clubs of New Jersey and Florida, the Nationals at Seattle, the great bridge playing country of Holland, the scenic mountains of Italy, and the World Championships in Chile. Wherever I go, the LAW is always with me.

APPENDIX A - BOLS TIP - 1993

When I was a young kid, just learning the game of bridge, my grandfather told me: "Larry, just follow a few simple maxims and you will go far." Second hand low, third hand high, buy low sell high (oops, wrong game), and "8 ever, 9 never" were amongst his favorites.

Little did he know that I would twist that last maxim around and use it as one of the keys to my success. What he taught me was always ("ever") finesse for the queen with eight trumps, and "never" finesse with nine. I went on to learn the LAW of Total Tricks, and that is when I discovered "EIGHT NEVER and NINE EVER!"

In this new "golden rule," the numbers 8 and 9 refer to the number of trumps in the combined hands of the partnership. If there is a 6-2 fit there are eight trumps, a 5-4 fit means nine trumps. The words "never" and "ever" refer to the act of competing (or bidding) on the three level on partscore hands.

"Eight never" means that you should never outbid the opponents on the three level if your side has only eight trumps. Conversely, "Nine ever" suggest that in the same circumstances with nine trumps you should "ever" and always compete to three of your trump suit.

Let's try a few hands. Nobody vulnerable, with:

♠ K Q 9 8 7 ♡ A 8 ◊ A 9 2 ♣ 10 7 2,

playing five-card majors, you deal and open one spade.
After a two-heart overcall, your partner raises to two
spades. Your RHO bids three hearts, and it is your
call. Your have a nice opening bid, but you should
not be tempted to bid three spades. Your side rates
to have only eight trumps -- so NEVER bid three-
over-three. If partner has four trumps, giving your
side nine, he will know to bid three spades. The full
deal rates to be something like:

```
                    ♠ A 6 3
                    ♡ 7 6 3
                    ◊ K 8 6 4
                    ♣ J 9 4
    ♠ 10 4                        ♠ J 5 2
    ♡ K Q 10 9 5                  ♡ J 4 2
    ◊ 10 5 3                      ◊ Q J 7
    ♣ A Q 3                       ♣ K 8 6 5
                    ♠ K Q 9 8 7
                    ♡ A 8
                    ◊ A 9 2
                    ♣ 10 7 2
```

The opponents were due to fail in three hearts, losing
five top tricks. You'll also fail if you bid three spades, as
you have five sure losers after the obvious heart lead.
Does this full deal contain anything surprising?

No, it is a very typical layout for this everyday auction. Both partnerships have an eight-card fit, and both sides can only take eight tricks. Why should you go minus when they are going minus?

If you were to give yourself a sixth spade, you would have a clear reason to compete to three spades. Let's even take away some high-card points to illustrate that possession of nine trumps is crucial -- not possession of an extra jack or queen. Holding:

♠ K98752 ♡ A8 ◇ A92 ♣ 107,

you are faced with the same auction as above. Your partner has raised spades, and the opponents have competed to three hearts. This time your side has nine trumps: NINE EVER -- so you bid three spades, expecting the full deal to resemble:

```
                ♠ A63
                ♡ 763
                ◇ K864
                ♣ J94
    ♠ 104                    ♠ QJ
    ♡ KQ1095                 ♡ J42
    ◇ 1053                   ◇ QJ7
    ♣ AQ3                    ♣ K8652
                ♠ K98752
                ♡ A8
                ◇ A92
                ♣ 107
```

Three hearts is still down one, but now you can make three spades. Your ninth spade translated into a ninth trick. What if the spades were 3-1? You'd go down, but then three hearts would make.

Why does this "eight never, nine ever" work out so well? The reason is simple if you know the LAW of Total Tricks, a concept which has only recently received the attention it deserves. The LAW states that the number of total trumps (add both side's best fit together) is approximately equal to the number of total tricks (add the number of tricks that both sides can take in their best suit). If the high cards are evenly split, eight trumps usually lead to eight tricks, and nine trumps usually lead to nine tricks. This is an oversimplification, but the concept is a sound one.

Over and over again, throughout the bridge world people bid "three-over-three" with only eight trumps, only to find that both three-level contracts fail. Instead of going +50 or +100, players go minus that same number.

I have given my self-learned advice to my grandfather and now he's the king of the senior circuit. He simply follows the reversed golden rule: "Eight never, Nine ever."

APPENDIX B - METHODS

Methods to get to our proper LAW Level

1) BERGEN RAISES: Conventional means of raising a one-heart or one-spade opening to the proper LAW level. Designed to tell partner our strength and, more importantly, our number of trumps.

2) PREEMPTIVE RAISES: Designed to get us to the proper LAW level in competition.

3) JACOBY TRANSFER - JUMP RESPONSES: For getting to the three level immediately with 9+ trumps.

4) D.O.N.T.: Best method for competing over opponents' one notrump opening. Gives ability to show all one and two-suiters at a safe level.

5) SUPPORT DOUBLES: Conventional method to show partner three-card support for the suit he has responded in.

6) UNUSUAL 1NT: Use of a one-notrump overcall for takeout of the two unbid suits to enable the finding of a fit at a safe level.

7) TWO-WAY DRURY: Use of both two clubs and two diamonds to show three or four-card support.

<u>Methods we use for keeping the opponents from playing on the two level with an eight-card fit:</u>

1) OBAR BIDS - Systemic approach to allow for "**B**alancing **I**n **D**irect **S**eat after the **O**pponents **B**id **A**nd **R**aise."

2) SCRAMBLING 2NT - Systemic approach whereby two notrump is used as an artificial way to "scramble" into the correct contract.

3) "SUPER" UNUSUAL 2NT - Use of two no-trump to show any two-suit takeout.

4) GOOD-BAD 2NT - Conventional method (similar to Lebensohl) which enables three-level competition with minimums.

5) AGGRESSIVE MINOR-SUIT RAISES - Recognition of the need to get quickly past two-of-their-major.

All of these methods were explained in detail in *To Bid or Not to Bid.*

APPENDIX C - RESPONSES TO DONT

RESPONDING TO DONT OVERCALLS WITHOUT GAME INTEREST (99% of the time!)

The overriding concept is safety. Try to play in any undoubled contract. Don't worry about getting to the *best* spot -- just try to get to any playable spot.

A) Partner overcalls two clubs (♣ + any other suit)

1) With three or more clubs, you should almost always pass.

Exception: With 4x3 (not four clubs), you might choose to bid two diamonds and try to play in partner's other suit -- hoping for a 4-4 fit. He will pass two diamonds if that is his other suit, or pull to his major.

2) With two or fewer clubs, you should almost always pull.

Exception: With a two-suiter of your own (say 5-5) and a doubleton club, you might guess to pass in fear (expectation) that partner's other suit is your singleton!

3) If you <u>pull to two diamonds</u>, partner will pass with diamonds as his second suit. So, you should have at least as many diamonds as clubs. Some examples (all patterns are in normal order ♠, ♡, ◇, ♣):

4-4-3-2: Pull to two diamonds - you'll play in diamonds if that is partner's other suit, or even better, in his major if he has one.

4-5-2-2 or 5-4-2-2: Pull to two diamonds (hoping for a major - but opposite the expected minors it's no big deal which two-carder you play in)

5-5-2-1: Pull to two diamonds - maybe you'll get lucky and partner will have a major!

5-4-3-1: Pull to two diamonds, of course.

4) If you <u>pull to two hearts</u> things are a bit confusing. Is it your own heart suit or is it a pass/convert type bid? Experience shows that it is best to treat this as responder's own heart suit.

5) <u>Pulling to two spades</u>. Definitely responder's own spade suit.

6) <u>Two notrump response</u> is covered at the end of this section.

7) <u>Raise to three clubs</u> - preemptive!

8) <u>Three of a new suit</u> - responder's own suit - invitational.

B) <u>Partner overcalls two diamonds ($\Diamond$ + Major)</u>

1) With three or more diamonds, you will usually pass, unless you have at least three in each major! (in which case you can venture two hearts.)

2) With two diamonds you will sometimes have to pass - especially if you fear a misfit:

5-1-2-5: I would pass two diamonds, fearing a red two-suiter.

4-2-2-5: You can risk two hearts, but only a real optimist would expect that partner's major is spades! You might want to stay put in two diamonds undoubled for the time being.

3) <u>Pulling to two hearts</u> asks partner to pass with red suits and pull to two spades with diamonds and spades. You might risk two hearts with, say, 2-4-4-3. If partner bid two spades, you can retreat to three diamonds.

4) Bids in <u>new suits</u> starting with two spades are

responder's own suits.

5) Two notrump response is covered at the end of this section.

6) A raise to three diamonds is preemptive.

C) Partner overcalls two hearts (majors)

With equal length in the majors you can pull to two spades if you want to put the notrump bidder on lead (usually a good idea). If your partner plays the dummy better than you (unlikely), you can choose to pass. Bids of three-of-a-major are preemptive. With game interest you would start with two notrump.

RESPONDING TO DONT OVERCALLS WITH GAME INTEREST (1% of the time!)

The responder, with game interest, can bid 2NT to ask for more information.

A) <u>After a two-club overcall (♣ + any suit) and 2NT ask:</u>

1) 3♣ = all minimums
(after which, 3♢ = pass/correct to other suit)

2) 3♢/♡/♠ = that suit and a maximum

B) <u>After a two-diamond overcall (♢ + either major) and 2NT ask:</u>

1) 3♣ = diamonds + hearts, minimum
2) 3♢ = diamonds + spades, minimum
3) 3♡/3♠ = diamonds + that major and a maximum

C) <u>After a two-heart overcall (majors) and 2NT ask:</u>

1) 3♣ = minimum, longer/better hearts
2) 3♢ = minimum, longer/better spades
3) 3♡/♠ = maximums, longer/better in suit bid

THE DONT OVERCALL IS DOUBLED

When you make a DONT overcall, and the opponents double, it is important to have partnership understandings. I suggest that after a double, you play that:

Pass = Tolerance for the suit overcalled - presumably the same call you would have made without the double.

Redouble = Asks overcaller for his other suit!

New suit = Responder's own suit. Note that this is potentially different from an auction in which there was no double:

   1NT - (2♣) - Dbl: 2 ◇ is now responder's own suit - not an ask for the overcaller's other suit!